PAUL REVERE AND THE MINUTE MEN

"*The ship took more than a month to get here.*" (p. 11)

PAUL REVERE

AND

THE MINUTE MEN

by **DOROTHY CANFIELD FISHER**

Illustrated by **NORMAN PRICE**

Landmark BOOKS

RANDOM HOUSE · NEW YORK

CONTENTS

PART I

The Apprentice

Paul and His Frenchie Father

1

IT WAS almost exactly two hundred years ago, but don't think that boys were not boys then. To go swimming in hot weather was just as much fun as now. And old Boston of 1746 had ever so many docks reaching out into good swimming water. There were long high ones where great merchant ships came sailing in from all over the world. Tall teen-age apprentice boys dived from them. And there were short, tumble-downish ones

3

where light fishing boats tied up. These were just right for smaller boys to paddle around while they got the hang of swimming.

The group of boys who were sunning themselves on the low Hitchbourn wharf were all small except one, who had gone along to take care of his little brother. They still had to let themselves down cautiously into the water, holding on. No diving yet for them. But they were big enough to brag about their folks and tell tall tales about the wild things that had happened to their fathers and older brothers and grandfathers. All children heard lots of old-timey stories at home in those days, for there were few books. Even if there had been plenty, there was very little light to read them by, come twilight and darkness. One candle on the mantel, and the flash of fire from the hearth—not many homes had more.

All the better for story-telling, of course. Boys could not be expected to do any active work when there wasn't light enough to see. They often set their wooden stools close around their grandmother, knitting, or their great-uncle, smoking his pipe, and asked for a tale. Like all boys they liked the exciting ones best. Those were what they were swapping on the wharf, that sunny summer day.

"My grandmother was out berrying, and met a great black bear, walking straight down the path towards her."

"What did she do?"

"She flung her wooden berry pail at its head and

screamed and bellered. The bear swung to and fro a minute and then went off, cross-lots."

"Once, when my grandfather was out ploughing, his dog barked and barked and he saw Injuns off in the bushes. He pretended he didn't see, and went on holding his plough to the end of the row, where he'd left his musket and powder horn. He grabbed it up, unhitched his horse from the plough, and started back to the house. The Indians began shooting their arrows. But they fell short. My grandfather kept shooting and loading all the way down the lane. He held them off till he got to the house. My grandmother had heard him shooting. She had the heavy shutters fastened over the windows and held the door open for him. He took the horse right in with him to keep it safe. And my grandmother slammed the door shut and pulled the bar to lock it. He stuck the barrel of his musket out through a hole and she did the same thing with another musket at the back. But the Indians didn't come, once they saw the house shut up and the barrels of the muskets showing. They went along. They weren't a war party with French officers. Just out hunting, probably, Grandfather said."

"My father was asleep in the loft of a house when it caught afire. He busted a hole out near the chimbley, got through and jumped into a tree that stood near by. An apple tree, 'twas."

"My great-grandfather was impudent to old Governor Endicott—sauced him right to his face." It was one of the smaller boys who made this brag.

The oldest one of the gang said, drowsily, "It was your great-great-grandfather, Tom. The Governor slapped his face for it, too. You didn't tell that."

"What do *you* know about it, Paul? Happened a hundred years ago. And your father is a . . ."

Paul sat up, quickly.

"Thomas Dexter was my great-great grandfather as much as yours," he said. He spoke offhand and easy, as though he didn't care much about it. But he went on, "My mother was a Hitchbourn. My grandmother owns this wharf." He looked over the edge of the dock, where a man was rowing a boat. "Halloo out there, Dick!" he shouted to the man. "Give us a tow, will you?"

The man good-naturedly backed water till the four small boys and the bigger Paul could let themselves down. Puffing and splashing, they paddled out to the boat. There they hung on the stern and floated out behind as the oarsman rowed forward, till Paul said, "That's far enough. Let go, everybody."

For them, with their short, little-boy strokes it was quite a swim. Paul saw to it that everybody got safely back to the dock. His small brother began to be tired. He breathed hard and sank lower and lower in the water. Paul swam back to him and said, "Hang on, Tom. I'll tow you in." When they climbed up, they were out of breath, and lay down in the sun again. It warmed them all over, for nobody in those days expected boys who went swimming off docks to wear bathing suits. This was just as well, for they hadn't any.

They went back to their tall stories. "My grandfather killed three Injuns in a fight, with nobody to
help him."

"My father walked twenty miles in one day in his
bare feet, when he was fourteen years old."

"One of my cousins got drownded off this very
wharf."

"When my grandfather was a boy, he worked in
Connecticut for an old man who had been on Cromwell's side in England, and had voted to cut the King's
head off."

Most of them had heard about that. Not from books,
for they weren't rich men's boys who studied history
and Latin. Their school only taught reading and writing and arithmetic. But their fathers had heard their
grandfathers tell about King Charles of England who
tried to make Englishmen do what *he* wanted, law or
no law. That story was one of those their fathers had
passed on to them, so they knew that Cromwell was
the general of the army that fought against the King.
They remembered it better than some of the other old-
time stories, for what boy is not interested in somebody's head being cut off? And the King's—! It was
something to think about—that a king's neck could be
chopped through by an axe just like anybody's, just
like a hen's. Yes, this story was the most important-
sounding so far.

Would anybody fish up a bigger one? A little boy
took the dare. He swallowed hard, and brought out
something really awful. "My Uncle Benjamin Frank-

lin broke his apprentice indentures and ran away from his master when he was seventeen."

This was a shock. They all stopped gabbling to stare. For a boy to break his indentures as an apprentice was, in those days, a good deal like forging a check nowadays.

Being an apprentice was serious. The only chance an ordinary boy had to earn his living was in a trade. And his only chance to learn a trade was to be taken in as student by a master-workman, who would teach him how to be a carpenter, a tailor, a butcher, a silversmith, a blacksmith. In those days, everybody (except from the few rich families) was apprenticed to some good workman when he was thirteen or fourteen years old. The master-workman had to promise to give the boy food, clothing and a place to sleep till he was twenty-one or so. On his side the boy had to promise to work for nothing for seven years (or longer) while he learned the trade. Of course, for the first few years his work wasn't worth much. So somebody in the family—his father, or uncle, or older brother—had to hand over good money to the master-workman to pay for what the student or apprentice cost. If the boy ran away from the man he was apprenticed to before the time he and his family had promised in the indentures, or agreement, it was the same thing as stealing money. And respectable families didn't raise boys who stole money.

Some of them had already heard about Benjamin Franklin's breaking his indentures. But it wasn't the kind of thing you talked about. They looked so embarrassed that Ned said, hastily, "Uncle Ben got to be a master printer in Philadelphia. He's making good money. Folks there call him a leading citizen."

But he could see that this didn't begin to make up for having a boy in the family who had broken the promises made when he was indentured. He thought to himself, "I'll pick on Paul, and give them something else to think about." Aloud he said, "Paul, you don't say anything about your Frenchie father. What did *he* ever do?"

They all knew Mr. Revere as a quiet man who went to church every Sunday, and who didn't have much to say in the hullabaloo of the noisy Hitchbourn family he had married into.

Paul looked quickly over at his little brother Thomas. The child was hanging his head, as if he felt ashamed. His face was flushed and shadowed. The older boy rolled over on his back, put his hands under his head and thought. Then he drew a long breath. "I'll tell you what he did. His folks in France lived in a big square stone house" (most of the Massachusetts houses were made of wood, so this sounded fine) "and there was a tall stone wall built all around the house and their garden and orchards. They had plenty of money. They had plenty of land. They were educated folks, they read books, they wrote a good hand. It was a fine, warm place where flowers were in bloom nearly all the year around.

"He could have stayed right there and owned all

that when he grew up. But if he did, he'd have had to pretend to believe in the religion the government wanted everybody to belong to, not the Church his father and mother and grandfather and grandmother went to. He knew all about this, from the time he was little.

"When he was twelve years old—that's just a year older than I am now—they all decided the best thing was for him to go to live with his Uncle Simon. This uncle had run away from France years before, when he was a boy, so he could go on belonging to the Church he and his family believed in. He lived on an island where the folks speak French, but it belonged to England. And——" Paul rolled over and looked hard at a boy, "you talk about your grandfather who one time worked for a man who voted to cut the King's head off. Listen! Everybody on that island was on Cromwell's side. My father told me that every chance they had, they stood up for the men in England who fought against the King."

He glanced again at little Thomas, lay back, rubbed his head, went on: "But just about the time when my father was to go to the island, his Uncle Simon wrote his father that the English laws were changed so that folks who didn't belong to the Church of the British government weren't to be let to teach their own children what they believed in."

This did not surprise the boys. In those days nearly everybody expected to have only one kind of religion in each nation. In almost all countries, people who didn't belong to the government Church were badly treated.

"My father was twelve years old. He and his folks talked it over and thought the only thing for him to do was to go to Boston. So he went first to the island, Guernsey. There his Uncle Simon paid for apprenticing him to a silversmith here, Mr. Coney, and paid for his passage. A few days after his thirteenth birthday my father started off by himself.

"The ship took more than a month to get here. When it came in, it tied up to Long Wharf, right over there——" he pointed. "Look, Thomas, don't you ever forget this. It's something for us Reveres to brag about. It was in the middle of winter. He'd been seasick, and still felt sort of weak. He didn't know a soul in Boston. He didn't know a word of English except 'yes' and 'no'. He didn't know what kind of a family he was going to work for. For all he'd ever heard about America they might be savages with feathers in their hair.

"Well sir, when he got off the ship and stood on Long Wharf, his legs felt as though they hadn't any bones in them. They felt as limp as cotton string. He's told me how they felt. I'm named for him; he tells me lots of things. But he stiffened his legs the best he could and marched up the street to Mr. Coney's house. By the time he got there he was shivering all over. For he hadn't any winter shoes or clothes, just what you'd have in a warm place where there was never any snow or ice. But he gritted his teeth to keep them from chattering, knocked on the door, and held his head up.

"When the door opened he remembered to take his cap off, for he'd been brought up to be mannerly. He was just a little boy, all alone, but he told me his father had told him, 'As long as there is a fighting chance, just one, a person can stand up and go on.' And he's stood up and gone on, ever since. *He* didn't break his indentures. And he kept every promise he ever made. He learned to be as fine a silversmith as there is in Boston —that is, since Mr. Coney died. He has his own shop now and takes care of his family and supports the Church. That's what Apollos Rivoire did. And, would anybody ask *me*, I'd say that's as good as being in a house when it caught a-fire, or getting drowned off a dock——" He turned his head, saw a boat being rowed by the wharf and shouted, "Halloo out there, Peter, give us a tow?"

They were off for another water adventure.

A Church Steeple and Some Rough Night Fun in the Streets

2

WHEN Paul Revere was growing up in Boston, it was not a big city. If you happen to live anywhere near Milford, Connecticut, or Gainesville, Florida, or Lawrence, Kansas, or Rutland, Vermont, or Idaho Falls, Idaho, you know how big, for Boston then had about as many people as those towns have now. And it wasn't spread out thin, as most of our cities are now, with big public parks and with the houses set far enough apart to have lawns and gardens around them. And it didn't stretch out into the country with suburbs. Boston was on an island. Well, at high tide it was, for the ocean flowed in over the neck which connected it with the mainland. You can't spread out over the edge of an island as you can on the prairie.

Boston houses were squeezed so tightly together that the noises of the city could be heard from anywhere. Especially the church bells. There were lots of these. Every church had its steeple, every steeple had its bell. People with good ears for musical tones could tell one bell from another by the sound. Paul did not have an especially keen ear for music, but he recognized the voice of one church when its steeple began to speak, for it had eight bells, not just one.

In those days Americans didn't have much metal, and they made as many things as they could out of wood. But you can't make a bell out of anything but metal. And Paul was especially interested in anything made of metal. He wondered how anything so big as a church bell could be cast.

In those days, there weren't any banks. Sometimes people put the silver coins they saved in an old sock, shoved that under a mattress, and kept their eye on the mattress for fear of thieves. Others hired a man who worked in silver to turn their coins into cups, spoons, dishes to eat cereal out of, and bowls. They got some use of the metal that way. If they needed cash-money afterwards, why, anybody could melt their cups or bowls back into plain silver. Silversmiths were needed. It was a good trade.

When he was still quite little, Paul learned a good deal about that trade, "through his pores," as people say. For the shop where his father worked was right in the house, so from the time he was a baby, Paul saw and heard what was going on there. When he heard, from his mother's busy kitchen, a pretty-sounding clink, clink, clink, he would crawl in on all fours to see what was making that interesting noise. If he were quiet, and crept into a corner out of the way, his father let him stay and watch the hammers beating out the plates or spoons, and see the red-hot charcoal fire where, over and over, the silver was heated to keep it soft enough to beat it into shape.

By the time he was a square-shouldered boy of thirteen, Paul was old enough (as people thought then) to be an apprentice. He started learning his father's trade, as his father had begun to learn it thirty-three years before on that cold winter's day when the ship from across the ocean tied up at Long Wharf.

Paul soon found out that he loved the trade he was learning. All his life long, he liked nothing better than to make things in silver. This was the best of luck for him. Nobody can have any better luck than to like the work he does to earn a living. But that didn't mean that as a boy he wasn't a great hand for going swimming in summer, or, come November, for whooping it up at a Guy Fawkes' night procession.

Guy Fawkes' night was on the 5th of November.
For Boston boys then, it was a good deal like our noisy
Hallowe'en goings-on, now. It was like Hallowe'en too,
because most people who celebrated it had no idea
what it meant. Hallowe'en began hundreds of years
ago. Everybody then believed that on the night of October 31st, ghosts of dead people got up out of their
graves, some in white sheets, some just in their bones,
as skeletons, and went around looking in through windows and trying to harm people who were still alive.
Many boys and girls today never heard of that idea!
All the same, on that night you like to put on queer
clothes—often white sheets, sometimes costumes that
make you look like a skeleton—and go out to make a
lot of noise and perhaps build bonfires.

Well, people in old Boston didn't think much about
the story of Guy Fawkes, and many of the boys probably didn't know there was any story. Yet every November 5th they had a big celebration. In the daytime,
the younger boys put on funny-looking clothes and carried around on the streets little stuffed figures dressed
up outlandishly to look like devils, witches and what
not. But at night, the bigger boys, the apprentices, took
over. Lots of grownups, too. They had horses drawing
a big wagon, with strange, made-up figures on it. Boys
hidden under the floor of the float worked strings so
that these great figures nodded their heads and spread
out their arms. It was fun for a boy to do that. But it
was much more fun to be out where you could see the
torches and the lanterns and run along behind the

wagon, blowing horns, beating on a drum or just screeching at the top of your voice. It was *one* time when nobody told you to shut up and keep quiet. The more noise you made, the better.

Nowadays, on the evening of October 31st, you put on queer clothes, grab a horn and go out to race up and down the streets, making soap marks on windows or ringing door bells. You don't do it to pretend you are a dead person, come to life. You do it just for fun. For the Boston crowds when Paul Revere was growing up, Guy Fawkes' day was just fun.

They had more than one kind of fun out of it. Once in so often, when everybody in the parade was out of breath, the procession used to stop before a house. Then the people living in the house were supposed to bring out all kinds of good things to eat and drink. The men let the boys reach up and grab their share. They had a right to. They had made a lot of the noise. Everybody likes to eat.

The end of the celebration was fun, too, but scaring fun. This was a fight, when one procession met another one like it from the other end of town. The two crowds were expected to mix it up fiercely. And they did. Each side tried to pull the devil and the other figures off the other float and tear them to pieces.

By that time of the night, the men had had a good deal to drink. They were tough customers anyhow, wharf workers, sailors, barrel-makers and big rough boys. The fight was a regular ruckus, a free-for-all, with clubs banging down, fists slugging, clothes torn off, people slammed off the floats and landing on their heads. Fathers and mothers told their boys to come straight home the minute the two processions met and the fighting began. I won't say they always did. Would you? They hovered around the edge of the fighting mob, far enough off to be safe—well, sort of safe—but near enough to hear and see. It was fun. But rough fun. One year a little boy was accidentally killed.

Of course boys from rich and stylish families didn't go out on Guy Fawkes' night. Such well-dressed boys weren't even allowed to look out. People who lived in fine houses were afraid of the rough goings-on, and early that night closed their big shutters tightly and locked their doors. Young Paul Revere, racing along with the big tough crowd, in his rough-and-ready work-clothes, bang-whanging on a drum, tootling on a horn, or raising Cain with a bell, used sometimes to look up at the tightly closed houses, and feel sorry for the dressed-up boys inside. Was he glad *his* family didn't try to put on style! That was something he had no use for, then or ever. He never wanted to look as though he had more money than he really had.

But after all, the Guy Fawkes' day excitement, like Hallowe'en, came only once a year. For most Boston people, life went on quietly, because every day was filled with work. Work hours were much longer then than anybody nowadays would stand. In fact, there really weren't any daylight hours that were not "working hours." People began their work as soon as it was light enough to see, and kept at it (except Sundays, of course) till twilight. Yet life wasn't so hard as you might think. There wasn't any special quitting hour, so they didn't have to hurry to get things done by the time a clock struck. They didn't hustle, probably never felt they had to hit it up and step lively to make up for lost time or to catch a bus the way we do every day.

But most of all, that way to live wasn't as hard as it sounds because the workshops, like Mr. Revere's, were generally right at home. Everybody knew what was being done, both in workshop and kitchen. The men were not 'way off, far from their families. If the house caught fire, the men were on the spot to put it out; and they were right there to help bring up the children. As he stood before his forge, holding a piece of silver in the flame to soften it, Paul Revere's father could call over his shoulder, "Come take a hand blowing the bellows, will you?" or, "You Paul, stop that! Help your mother carry the water in." Or, "Halloo there, Paul and Thomas, don't you want to see me solder the handles on this bowl?" The fathers knew as well as the mothers what the children were up to.

When Paul was an apprentice in his 'teens, he had an idea about the Christ Church bells. He wanted to learn how to ring them, and he also wanted to earn some pocket-money by an extra job, the way many boys do. But of course he couldn't do it alone. There were eight of those big bells. Fortunately he always got on well with other people. This is another piece of good luck for anybody. He was about the Boy Scout age, when boys like to get up clubs and belong to gangs. With six other boys he knew and liked, he organized a "society," as they called it, to take on the job of ringing those bells.

They put their heads together and made up a set of rules for themselves. True American-style rules they were. They elected a president, or chairman. They called him the "moderator." And they voted in a new one every three months. This was to make sure that no moderator tried to have things too much his own way. Another rule was that new members (up to eight) were to be voted on and taken in only if everybody voted for them. Any member who broke the rules should be expelled. All questions were to be settled by a vote of the members present. You couldn't think up any better rules for any club, nowadays.

So now, one evening a week, Paul's society (nowadays you might call it his gang) went to the Church to learn how to ring the chimes. The evening was the only free time they had, for all the boys were in their teens, and that was the age when boys worked all day long, every single day, learning a trade.

In midsummer, evenings are still light. After they had climbed the long steep stairs of the tower up to where the bell-ropes hung, they could still see off over Boston. Paul had good sharp eyes (even if his ears were not very accurate on music) and he must have come to know where everything was in the wide scene he looked out upon. The Charles River on one side, Bunker's Hill, Foster's Hill, the Harbor, the big green open field called "The Common."

It was the only time those city boys were ever so high in the air. They probably did what we all do when we look off from a height—tried to see if they could pick out the houses they lived in, tried to tell one wharf from another. They often had words over whether a ship coming up the Harbor was a tall merchantman, or a whaler. They watched the ferry going across to Charlestown.

I wouldn't say that they didn't sometimes lean out and spit down to see where the spit fell, but the tower was so high they couldn't be sure. Every summer evening before they settled down to work, they always took a good long look all around, from every side of the tower.

Like most city boys in those days, Paul hardly ever left the paved town streets. Why would he? But looking off from the tall church tower, he learned what lay outside Boston. He became a good map-maker later on. Maybe he got the idea from looking down on Boston and the country and the water around it. He could have shut his eyes and told you where everything was as you saw it from the tower—the river, the harbor, the roads. Many times down in the street, he liked to look up and see the steeple of Christ Church, tall above the houses. He knew that you could see a long way from the top of it. And it was easy to figure out that it could be seen from a long way off, too.

As you read about what Paul Revere did years later, when he was a man grown, don't forget the many evenings when he and his gang of apprentice-boy friends climbed up those steep steps to the top of that tall tower.

While you are about it, don't forget those rough Guy Fawkes mobs, yelling and marching with torches, and blacking their faces till they scared the rich people to lock up their fine houses. You'd hardly think it, but they too, like the tall steeple, had something to do with the American Revolution.

Things Are Quiet for a While

3

FROM the beginning of his teens on, till he was a young man of nineteen, Paul Revere's days were mostly made up of long hours of work. But it was work he loved to do, and he enjoyed getting better and better at it. You know how boys who care a lot about tennis, or their stroke at swimming, or ski-turns, work their heads off to improve, from the time they're thirteen till they leave college. Paul worked that way at

silversmithing, with his father for coach. Everybody
wanted him to do just one thing during those 'teen
years of his, to learn how to be a good silversmith.
That was all right for Paul, because that was what he
himself most wanted to do. I told you he was lucky, or
anyhow, that he knew how to take hold of life, as
sensible people take hold of a poker, by the handle and
not by the hot end.

Paul and his younger brother Thomas were both
apprenticed to their father. They were close to him in
the same small shop, month after month, year after
year, long hours every day. They didn't work at different benches, the way men in an office sit at different
desks, or in separate rooms. Mostly they stood close
together, as they turned a flat piece of silver into a tray
or a rounded buckle, or a deep cup. One held the silver
in the fire just the right length of time; another maybe
would be blowing the bellows to get the charcoal burn-
ing red; the other stood by to hand exactly the hammer
or the engraving-tool needed.

No men or boys ever lived who could work together
as closely as that for as many years without coming to
know each other very well, even if one of them is as
quiet a man as Apollos Rivoire was. (By that time his
name had been shortened in American talk to Paul
Revere. He evidently liked it that way, for that was
what he named his oldest son, Paul Revere.) Naturally,
working side by side with his father, handing him his
tools, asking him how deep to engrave a line, how to

know when the silver was soft enough to handle, the younger Paul came to know every trade secret his father had learned from old Mr. Coney. By the time he was in his middle 'teens, he did as good work as his father. Later on, as he was close to twenty, he did better.

Perhaps this was because he had had a happier boyhood than the homeless little French boy who had to learn not only his trade but also how to speak English and how to put up with Yankee cooking. Paul turned out to have a gift for modeling the wax moulds in which the melted silver was poured when a big piece was cast. Some very fine sculptors have begun by being silversmiths. Perhaps Paul's father remembered hearing about them in France. He was twelve, you know, before he had to flee away from his good home there. In those days children were older for their years than now, and heard a great deal of serious talk by the time they were twelve. In the long hours he worked with his skillful, broad-shouldered, cheerful, kind-hearted son, Mr. Revere had time to pass on to him not only all he knew about making silver spoons and cups, but also many memories of his life in France. Paul may have heard a lot about the finely cut carvings on the beautiful stone buildings and homes and churches in France. Nothing very definite, probably. But more than boys with plain Yankee fathers and grandfathers ever dreamed of.

Anyhow we don't need anybody to tell us that it was a great comfort to Mr. Revere, when his time came to die, to have such a good son to carry his name on in the new world. For when Paul was nineteen, his father died. His widow lived to be very old; and those were the times when, as the tombstones show, life was so hard on women that many of them died young. So we can guess that Apollos' wife was happier and more kindly treated than many American women around her.

His son Paul wrote of Mr. Revere that he left "a good name and seven children." Not much money. But that didn't matter in a family when the eldest son was already a skillful, hardworking silversmith, just about ready to be a master-workman. The Reveres got along very well. At nineteen Paul was still indentured, and so couldn't run his own shop. But by Massachusetts law, his mother could carry on her husband's shop. Paul and his mother always got along peaceably, so he went right on at his father's bench though for a while he was supposed to be only his mother's helper. As apprentice, he had his brother, Thomas. A still younger brother was apprenticed to another trade. His older sister Deborah was soon to be married. Two other sisters were nice little girls helping Mrs. Revere do the housework. Paul always loved both his family and his trade. It seemed all right to him to go on working to earn the family living.

For nearly two years his life looked like the quietest kind of pool, still and smooth. But all at once, the current of the stream began to run fast again, and made a great swinging turn in a new direction.

One day a drum began to beat outside the door of the Revere house. What its rolling boom-boom-boom said to Paul decided a great many very important things for him. For us, also, over two hundred years later.

PART II

The Lieutenant

Apollos Rivoire's Son Goes to War

4

OF COURSE nobody knows exactly what happened at any special minute a hundred or two hundred years ago. How could we? But we do know what people did, year after year, every day. From that we can tell pretty certainly how they felt, and so how they acted, when something had to be done.

We know that the two Revere boys, Paul and Thomas, worked all day long, every day, side by side at the same bench. So we know that they stood there together when the rat-tat-tat of the drum sounded outside the door of the shop.

Thomas exclaimed, "What's that?" although he knew that the drum was calling for volunteers to fight the French and Indians. Every American man and boy knew that.

The colonial militia was like our National Guard, except that every man had to serve in it to get his military training. Every year the militia drilled on muster days in American villages and towns to be ready for home defense. But by law the militia couldn't be required to serve outside of American land. If soldiers were needed to fight the French and Indians in Canada, the men themselves could decide whether or not they would go. The drum of the muster-captain beating in Boston streets was asking them to go of their own free will.

"Rat-tat-tat," the drum called to Paul Revere, "rub-a-dub-dub. Will you fight or stay at home?"

Paul answered it by flinging down his hammer. "This time I'm going," he told his younger brother, setting his square jaw.

Thomas knew about the danger from Indian raiders led by the French in Canada. Not an American child of those days but heard terrible stories about Indians swooping down from the woods on a farmhouse, murdering the farmer, and capturing the women and bigger children to sell as slaves in Canada. If the babies were a bother, they were killed the way anybody'd step on a beetle.

Off and on, England and France had been at war ever since Apollos Rivoire had landed in Boston. As long as this kept up the American colonists knew they were in this horrible danger from the Indians.

But the Revere boys knew from their French father about another danger. They knew what would happen not from the Indians during the war, but from the French after the war if the French won. Not from studying about it in a history book, but because it had happened to their very own father and to his family. Paul and Thomas Revere knew what the French government did to people who did not want to belong to the French King's Church. Mr. Revere had told them that his father and mother had risked years of prison if the French police had found out that they had baptized their little son in their own Church.

As they blew the bellows to make their charcoal fire red, their father, waiting with a piece of silver in his tongs, used to tell them all kinds of stories his parents had told him. "If we lived in France, now," he'd say, "you children wouldn't have any legal rights, couldn't inherit anything from me, because the French law wouldn't admit that your mother and I are really married."

Sometimes his stories were darker. "One of my cousins was tortured in prison to make him give up his own Church. He died of it."

Other Boston boys, when they heard the drum-beat calling for recruits for the army, might think with a shudder of yelling Indians with tomahawks and scalping knives. The Revere boys thought of Indians, too. But, also with a shudder, they thought of fine, serious, hard-working French families, trying to escape from the French police and get into a free country, hiding by day, traveling by night.

Apollos Rivoire's two sons looked hard at each other. "Do you remember," asked Paul, "Father's saying that when his aunt's family first saw the mountains of Switzerland 'way off in the distance, they knelt down in the ploughed field they were crossing and thanked God that there *was* a place they could go to be free?"

Yes, Thomas nodded. All the Revere children had heard that story.

"Well," said Paul, reaching for his street coat, "this time if the French should win, over here, there wouldn't be any place for us to go to. Nowhere. Nowhere at all. We'd have to jump into the sea. I'm going to enlist. You're too young to. But I will."

Thomas's face had turned a deep, proud red. He looked at his older brother as if he were already a hero. "The next boy tells me we Reveres aren't really British, and want the French to win because our father was . . ."

"Knock him down!" said Paul enthusiastically.

"But Mother won't want to let you go," said Thomas anxiously.

"She will too. Do you suppose Father never told

her any of his stories about what happened in France? She knows as much as we do—more too, probably. She thought a lot of Father. He was always good to her. She'll know how we feel. She won't say a word against it."

Nor did she. The day in early May of 1756 when Paul marched away in his blue uniform, perhaps there were tears in her eyes, but they were not only because she was afraid she would never see her splendid oldest son again. They were tears of pride too. For Paul was an officer. This couldn't have happened in the English army because English officers were always from families with property. Paul was a man who worked with his hands. Yet, because this was an American army, he was not just a corporal or a sergeant, but a real officer with an officer's uniform, an officer's right to command his men, and a salary of thirty dollars a month, which sounded big in those days.

That this happened tells us a thing or two about the American Army as different from the British forces. It also shows what people thought of Paul Revere. Since Americans were free to enlist or not as they pleased in fighting French Canada, of course a lot was done to make them want to join the army. The privates themselves had a good deal to say about who were to be their officers. It's pretty plain that the boys who lived near the Reveres thought a good deal of Paul.

Mr. Revere had been dead less than two years when Paul left the work which all his life he liked better than anything else, when he left his mother to try to run the business and to take care of the younger children. His father's memory was very fresh in Paul's heart. When the young artillery lieutenant marching off to war at the head of his men looked back at his mother, he must have seen his well-remembered father too, shadowy but clear, and with a proud smile on his face.

Lieutenant Revere squared his broad shoulders, and stepped off with a quick firm step to the music of the high fifes and the booming roll of the drums. He certainly was glad he had enlisted. Not that he thought he was off to a spring holiday, with flags out on the houses and people running to see the troops go by, shouting to them "Go in and win," or whatever they said in those days that meant that. He knew better.

Paul always had plenty of common sense. He knew very well that a lot of the men in their new blue uniforms swinging along in the bright spring weather would be killed, and that he might be one of them. He knew he might be scalped by Indians, shot in battle, or poisoned by bad food. For in those days they didn't know how to preserve their rations, and what the soldiers had to eat was often mildewed and half rotten. He knew all that, but he also knew that he was doing what his father would want him to do. It was what had to be done, if he and his family were not to suffer as his father's family had.

Till now he hadn't thought much about such serious things. During his years as a hard-working apprentice, he was a boy, too young for politics, and he had been busy every minute with his beloved silver-working. But nobody, he felt, could have any doubts about whether to get in on *this* fight. Certainly nobody with a French name. Naturally a Revere understood what the fight was about better than a Perkins or a Dawson who had never heard what his French father had told him.

Dutch and Indians

_____

WITH horses and oxen hitched to cannon and supply wagons, the Massachusetts soldiers marched west. May is a fine month, the country was their own, everybody in the farmhouses, towns and villages was friendly. The day's march was never so long as to be tiring to active young men, because oxen walk very slowly. The soldiers had plenty of bounce left in them every afternoon when they stopped to make camp for the night. They had gay times with the folks who lived in each place. They were proud to be in the Massachusetts troops, and the Massachusetts people were proud of them.

Things were rather different when they left their

own colony at its far western end and marched to the Dutch village called Albany in New York Province. Here they were to meet other American troops. So they did. There were already troops from the other colonies. And lots more came in, soon after the Massachusetts men arrived.

Albany was the jumping-off place for fighting in the North Woods. Here the Colonial soldiers were to be met by the general who was to be in command. He would be, they all knew, a British officer. The British government took it for granted and supposed everybody else did, that of course no American officer knew enough to be in command of the troops of his own country. Certainly no American militia officer was good enough to give orders to *British* soldiers.

The Colonials were used to this, although they never pretended to like the idea. If the British general had been there at Albany to lead them on to fight, maybe they wouldn't have thought about it especially. But he wasn't. Other Colonial soldiers were milling around. No English commander. No English troops.

Nobody knew when the British general would arrive. They hadn't, you see, any telegraph, or telephone, or even any regular quick way to get letters sent. So nobody knew much about what was going to happen. Or, for that matter, what had happened anywhere, till long afterwards. Along with the troops from the other colonies, the soldiers from Massachusetts camped out around Albany to wait for General Loudoun to come. They waited and waited.

The people who lived in the village of Albany were

as Dutch as Dutch. They spoke Hollandish. Their church services were in the Dutch language. They looked blank if you spoke English to them. But the Massachusetts men thought the villagers knew quite enough English to ask five times a fair price for anything they had to sell. They were evidently good at making money this way, for they lived very well, in tight, well-built, snug homes, with nice little front porches where they sat on warm afternoons. The Massachusetts men had never seen front porches before. They had never been where the people didn't speak English.

Paul Revere was always interested in everything he saw, and at first he used to walk around in his spare time, noticing how these Dutch-speaking people managed life, keeping their house floors and windows and furniture scrubbed cleaner than he had ever seen, for all his mother was a good, tidy housekeeper.

There were Indians too, hanging around, camping out, off and on, down by the river, where they could fish. Paul had thought he would be interested to see Indians—real, wild Indians, not like the ragged clam-diggers from down Plymouth way. He kept looking for savage chieftains among those at Albany who came and went all the time, bringing furs to sell, or cloth they brought from Canada, for the Dutch merchants to sell at a big profit. But these were more like dirty tramps, and they smelled like rotten eggs. They didn't speak any English either, only a little Dutch and a little French. Paul didn't like them very well. But he was sorry for them, when he noticed that the Albany merchants double-crossed and cheated them as badly as they cheated the American soldiers. He didn't much blame them when they got wildly angry at the Dutch business people, nor when they ended by taking what money they could and getting disgustingly drunk on it.

There was excitement once in a while when a trapper or three or four woodsmen came in from the North Woods which stretched darkly between Albany and Canada. These men told terrifying stories about the French and Indian armed forces driving nearer and nearer to the American colonies, butchering anybody who got in their way.

There was always a commotion when a group of men in ragged buckskin clothes with long-barrelled hunting guns came into Albany, limping on sore feet in worn old moccasins, but thankful to get out of the North Woods alive. Lieutenant Revere dreaded seeing them. He knew beforehand what would happen.

First, they threw their tattered caps up in the air and shouted for joy, when they saw all those American troops in good uniforms with guns and cannons and plenty of ammunition, and pack-horses and ox-carts loaded with rations and tents. That warlike scene looked good to them. They had been for weeks in the black forest, in deadly danger from French and Indians every minute of the day and night. Men in their party had been killed by arrows or bullets that seemed to come, Injun-fashion, from nowhere. Most of them had lost everything they had. They hated the French and the Indians as much as they feared them. At their first sight of those American troops, ready to drive back the enemy, the ragged, half-starved woodsmen would let their flat knapsacks slide from their thin backs to shout "hip, hip, hurray!"

At this Lieutenant Revere felt queer. He knew very well the next thing would be the question, "When do you start north . . .?" Every time he heard that question he felt queerer. But he had to answer. He had to explain to these men, so happy that the American Army was going to fight for them, that the Americans had left their shops and farms and businesses in the spring to get a good early start for fighting. But then he had to add that they couldn't take a step till some Britishers got there from England to boss them.

"Well, where *is* the British general?"

Lieutenant Revere could only say, "He hasn't come yet."

"Why, don't the British care enough about the danger from Canada even to get here on time?" the woodsmen would cry.

Lieutenant Revere had no answer to make.

So they stuck it out in Albany as best they could, waiting and waiting, with nothing to do. And you know how it is when you're just hanging around with the gang, waiting for something to happen—it's hard to keep some of the boys out of mischief. When the young silversmith was made an officer, he had promised that he would keep the soldiers under his command "in good Order and Discipline." He had all he could do to keep them from running wild.

He himself was always interested in things made out of metal. He filled his own time learning what he could about the cannon. He was an artillery officer, you'll remember. He tried to figure out how the field artillery was cast, how it was put together, how it worked, how to keep it in good shape. What he learned about cannon that summer he used, some years later, to help along the American Revolution, as he used everything he ever learned to help the American side. But he couldn't expect the ordinary privates to take an interest in studying and learning. *Their* interest was to get started on what they had come to do. They wanted to fight for their country, not to hang around in the summer heat with a lot of Dutch-speaking Dutchmen and Indians who smelled enough to knock you down.

Lieutenant Revere couldn't, nobody could, drive the soldiers to keep themselves and their camp really clean, to drill faithfully on the parade ground in the hot summer sun, to dig holes deep enough to bury their garbage.

They hadn't enlisted, they told him, they told everybody, to march up and down a flat, open piece of land, nor yet to take care of garbage. They had enlisted to fight in the woods against an enemy threatening to ruin everything their fathers had built up for a hundred years. Young Lieutenant Revere could not talk the soldiers down very well, because he felt just as they did.

But anyhow, he thought as soon as General Loudoun and his fine staff appeared, everything would come to life. Compared to Colonial troops made up of men who worked for their living most of the time and soldiered only once in a while, the British officers and soldiers must know just about everything there was to know about waging war. They didn't do anything else all their lives. And their army had been at it for hundreds of years.

Like most of the younger Colonials in the troops there that summer, Paul had seen too few Englishmen really to know them. The English officials in Boston were so grand and elegant they had almost nothing to do with plain Americans like the Hitchbourns and Reveres. When they wanted to buy something, they usually sent a servant for it. When they did have to speak to a farmer or merchant, they hardly looked at him. The Governor of Massachusetts was always an Englishman. But who in Boston saw anything of the Governor except a glimpse of a splendidly dressed man in a big coach going by, on the street? None of the high British officials seemed to do any work—only draw big salaries, because they came from important families. When an ordinary Bostonian had business with one of the High Commissioners, he never saw him. More likely just his clerk, working long hours at a desk.

So Paul Revere looked forward with interest to the arrival of the English general and his British soldiers. He wanted to find out what kind of folks they were. And he thought he could learn a lot from them.

He often imagined, often told his exasperated men, what would happen soon after General Loudoun came. The tents would be packed up, the oxen yoked, the horses harnessed, the lines of soldiers formed tautly; the fife and drum would begin to squeal and away they would go. They'd show these Dutch shopkeepers who were laughing at them now that they were real soldiers.

Lieutenant Revere Comes to Know Some Englishmen

6

BY AND by the British general came. The officers with him were in beautifully tailored scarlet uniforms with lots of gold lace. The nine hundred British soldiers, specially picked to make a fine showing, were in scarlet too, but of course no gold lace. The young Colonials stared curiously at them as they marched into camp. Now, they thought, they were going to find out what English people were like.

The British troops were so well drilled that when they marched, you'd think you were watching one big machine, not a lot of human beings. Their legs all rose together, every knee bent at exactly the same angle, every foot came down, thump!! on the ground at exactly the same instant. They had drilled hard to be able to march like one big machine, not a lot of men, and they naturally thought the men from the shops and farms of Massachusetts would be very much impressed. Their proud, satisfied faces showed they expected to be admired.

They certainly did not admire the Americans! When in their turn the Colonial militia stepped off on the drill ground, the British couldn't keep from laughing out loud (not that they tried very hard) at the hop-skip and jump of the American lines. They did laugh out loud, and they said as loudly, that certainly General Loudoun would never lead into battle troops who couldn't drill any better than *that!*

Sure enough, the British general wrote the American general that the Americans didn't keep step at all well, nor even all go the same way the instant a command was given. You see, the English troops didn't have any work to do except to be soldiers, in peace times and war times. And, except in the American colonies, when they served outside of England they were always with other professional armies. They didn't know what to make of earning-a-living citizens, part-time soldiers like the American militia. The English general naturally wanted them to look more like the other soldiers he had known, and to act more like men who hadn't anything else to do but be army men. He said the Americans would have to practice drilling a lot more before he took them into the forest to fight. Also, they'd have to keep their uniforms neater, brush their hair more and polish their shoes and their buttons.

After losing so much time waiting for the British to get there, this made the soldiers as mad as hornets. Lieutenant Revere was mad himself, but being an officer, he couldn't say so to his soldiers. He had to try harder than ever to keep his men's spirits up, and get them to act more the way the British officers thought they ought.

The trouble was that he didn't really believe, any more than his men did, that bringing every foot down *thump!* at exactly the same instant would help much in fighting Indians in the woods. While they had been waiting around, he had met many young officers from other American colonies. From them he had heard about what had happened, just the summer before, to another British general—name of Braddock—who had come over from England and had taken British troops into the woods to fight Indians. Their buttons and their shoes were perfectly polished, their red uniforms didn't have a speck of dust on them, they could keep in step absolutely, their feet all struck the ground at the same instant, and the minute they got a command they wheeled in the same direction. But that was all the good it did them. For the Indians and French in buckskins, taking aim from behind trees, had shot them down the way duck hunters shoot into a flock of ducks. General Braddock had been killed almost right away, and so had most of his troops. If there hadn't been a young officer from the colony of Virginia—name of Washington—who knew what was needed, they might *all* have been killed.

Before the British general had arrived, the Colonial militia had had, as they waited around, lots of time on their hands to discuss things and compare notes with each other. The story of the terrible defeat of the British troops under General Braddock was told over and over, whenever the Americans, officers or privates, got together. With it went a piece of information which wasn't new, for it had happened two years before, but was new to younger officers like Paul Revere. This was the fact that the year before General Braddock came over with his red-coats, the War Office in London, where all the army rules came from, had sent out a statement saying that,

"Provincial officers of any rank should be subordinate to any officer holding the King's Commission."

This meant that a war-seasoned, much-honored American like old General Putnam of Connecticut, when he served with British troops, would have to obey the orders of any British officer, even a young lieutenant. And no British officer would obey him. Any Englishman was assumed to be better than any American.

Every time this order was spoken about at Albany while the militia were waiting around, it was with

anger. They liked the news that young Colonel Washington, when he heard that he was to be "subordinate to any British officer," resented it so hotly he just resigned from the militia altogether. That's what they would have done in his place. Colonel Washington had gone out with the English forces, that summer of the great British defeat, only because General Braddock said he specially needed him and specially invited him.

Lieutenant Paul Revere had the Braddock story very much in mind as he tried his best to get his rough-and-ready Boston boys to keep step and brush their hair and polish those darned buttons. He knew that, the year before, the young Virginia militia officer, George Washington, had tried to explain to General Braddock that keeping in step and brushing your hair wasn't what was most needed for fighting Indians in the thick, dark American woods. He knew that now in Albany their own militia officers, the older, higher-ranking ones, were trying to tell General Loudoun the same thing. But apparently British generals were too sure they were always right, to pay any attention to American militia who might be officers today but, as like as not, farmers tomorrow. "If one button on a man's coat wasn't shining," thought Paul, "nobody in the British Army could hear what he had to say."

But in a tight place, Paul often thought of his father at thirteen, still groggy with sea-sickness, stiffening his little legs against the cold, and marching up a strange street to a family who might be savages for all he knew. He was determined to keep going—and he did.

He drilled and drilled his men, all day. In the evening he talked with other young officers from Pennsyl-
vania and Connecticut and New York. That summer he
heard more about what was going on outside of Massachusetts than he had ever dreamed. At night he lay
down in his tent and tried to make some sense out of
what was happening around him.

There wasn't much sense to be made of it. There,
just over there, were the French, coming closer all the
time. Here were lots and lots of soldiers crazy to fight.
But the British general did nothing. "Might's well be a
picture of a general painted on a board," Paul heard
the men say grumblingly. That was what he thought
too. So he pretended not to hear them.

In this second period of waiting and waiting, Paul
tried to get more acquainted with the Englishmen in
the British forces. But it was not much of a success. Apparently, the English didn't want other people to get
acquainted with them. Paul was astonished to find that
although he and they spoke the same language, they
seemed more like foreigners to him than the Albany
Dutch. What little he saw of them he didn't like. There
were only three things the English officers seemed
to care about: drinking, playing cards, and betting. Their
tremendous bets took Paul Revere's breath away.
Where *did* they get the money to bet like that? The
American Colonials, with their modest monthly pay,
couldn't imagine. And as for their drinking, Paul
couldn't see that the English officers were any better
than those wretched Indians, who'd sell anything to

buy whiskey and then drink themselves dead, blind drunk.

Lieutenant Revere didn't like what they did, and he really hated the way they treated their own soldiers. They seemed to think any private was a slave to any officer. If they felt like it, they would have a soldier terribly whipped, hundreds of lashes, while they stood by, taking snuff and joking with each other. They called this "discipline".

But Paul was interested as he always was, all his life, in learning things. He didn't understand the reasons for some of the British drill regulations, and he still had the idea that the famous proud British officers must know a great deal more than he, just a common silversmith.

So one day, he walked up to a young British officer, at a time when the Englishman evidently didn't have anything special to do, for he was idly shuffling a pack of cards over and over.

"Lieutenant, may I ask a question about small arms drill?" Paul said. "One of your sergeants has just been showing our men how to load. He insists that they all take a step back, just so many inches, each one of them the same distance, with his left foot; then slant his musket at just the same angle with all the others. Now some men are much taller than others, some have shorter arms and legs. They'd ram their charges down a lot faster, it seems to me—but maybe I'm wrong—if they had a little leeway about getting the barrels of their muskets to a convenient height."

The British lieutenant looked up blankly at him. He stared. After a moment, he said, "What did you say?"

Paul Revere repeated, and said at the end, "I just thought, sir, I'd ask you *why* it's done that way."

The British officer kept on shuffling his cards for a while. Then he yawned, and said carelessly, as you'd speak to a troublesome child, "Because that's the *way* to do it."

Paul waited a minute. The other did not look up, nor show he knew Paul was there. Lieutenant Revere went back to his own tent, asking himself, "Did he answer that way just to be disagreeable? Or is he so stupid he doesn't know the reason?" He never found out which was the truth. But whichever it was, he didn't like it.

He counted the days, which got longer and hotter. Finally, General Loudoun's orders to move were sent out. The Massachusetts troops were to be sent up the Hudson a short distance, and then really—hurrah!— off north into the wild forest where the enemy was, up to Fort William Henry at the end of Lake George. It was about time! News had come in, alarming news, that while the English-speaking troops were marking time, the French and Indians had captured an important English fort, Oswego. The militia were in a greater hurry than ever to get into action. If Fort Oswego had been captured, the enemy might sweep right out of the woods and across the province of New York. Some of them thought that this summer's fighting would settle the matter one way or the other.

On the day they left Albany, the Massachusetts militia swung briskly into rank behind the fife and drum corps! How good it seemed to be moving again! The men, who had come to be so slack and disorderly, snapped into military style like soldiers. There was a fair road through the North Woods to Lake George. They covered it in good time and in high spirits. At last, heads up, uniforms clean, stepping in time to the drums, they swept into Fort William Henry.

Lieutenant Revere Gets a New Idea

7

WHAT followed next was like a long bad dream for Lieutenant Revere. For everybody. You won't believe it, but they just stayed there in the Fort.

Orders to move on and fight didn't come from head-quarters. Not then. Not at all. The men cut down trees by the hundreds, and made a fleet of boats to carry them on the lake. This was evidently so they could get near enough the French-held fort north of them to attack it. Those boats were never used.

Every day they expected a messenger from British headquarters to come in with the longed-for command to get out and fight. That command never came. They all hated the fort. Naturally, it was hard for the officers to make the men keep a place they hated clean and tidy. When you might be gone the next day, why clear up the mess left after slaughtering pigs for the regiment's dinner? The camp cooks threw their slops out anywhere, flies blackened the air, and nobody in those days had ever heard of boiling water to make it safe for drinking.

It wasn't long before there was a lot of sickness in the camp. Scarcely any of them felt well and strong. Every day about four hundred men (out of 2500) "reported sick." Every day four or five soldiers died. Day after day, a squad of half-sick men dug four or five graves for their dead friends and comrades. It was felt that the graves should be close at hand, to keep the wild animals from digging up the bodies to eat them. But the ground was stony and the grave-diggers, even the ones who weren't sick enough to have the camp doctor, hadn't strength enough to make the graves very deep. This didn't improve the smells around that wretched fort, that summer and autumn.

There was one smell, which they had thought a frightful one in Albany, but which they actually liked there in the woods by the lake. They soon found why the Indians smelled so. To protect themselves from the millions of mosquitoes, they smeared their skin with a thick layer of bear's grease—always plenty of that around in those days. In hot weather, grease turns rancid and smells like rotten eggs. But, as long as it hadn't rubbed off, it still kept the mosquitoes from stinging. The Massachusetts militia soon smelled as strong as any Indian. But since everybody did, nobody objected. They felt much obliged to those Indians at whom they had turned up their noses in Albany.

That summer was like a nightmare. They not only could not attack the French fort to the north of them, they could not even defend themselves from the attacks of the enemy. For every night they were fired on from the woods by the French and Indians. They'd sneak up in the dark, silent on their moccasined feet, pick off a few of the Massachusetts soldiers, and vanish in the thick, trackless forest. Sometimes little detachments of American militiamen were sent out at night to try to do the same thing back at the enemy. But they never could find where any French or Indians were camped. And the black-flies swarmed, there were millions of fiercely stinging mosquitoes in the night-woods, the wood-ticks crawled into every crack of the soldiers' clothing if they sat down for a moment, and bit like fury.

Lieutenant Revere wondered now why they had thought that waiting in Albany was tiresome. Would they ever again have such a good life as that? A great many of them never would, for they died, day by day, from bullets, knives or sickness. He raged as he saw Boston boys die, those he had known all his life, who had liked him so much they wanted him as their officer. These Boston friends of his who sickened and died, or whose corpses were brought into camp with bloody scalped heads—they were citizens, hard-working skillful artisans with a lifetime of usefulness before them. And they were nice young fellows whose anxious mothers and fathers were waiting for them back home. And what for? They might as well have stayed safely in Boston for all the good they'd done in this war.

What did it mean? What could it mean? Sometimes he thought he had lost his mind, that clear, sensible mind he had always counted on. Try as he might, Lieutenant Revere could not understand a single bit of what was happening.

Of course he wasn't the only American in that camp to wonder what in this world they were supposed to be doing. Everybody asked the same question— "What's the sense to all this?"

By the end of August there was less heat. The first frosts came early in September. That killed off the mosquitoes. But not the stealthy raids from invisible scattered French and Indian sharpshooters.

Nights grew colder. The light-weight, spring-weather uniforms that the Massachusetts men had worn as they left Boston in May were still all they had. No winter supplies were brought in. Shivering over the small campfires, starting at every sound from the dense woods around them, the militiamen said loudly, "This whole business doesn't make sense. What did they get us out *for*?"

Lieutenant Revere's face hardened. He said nothing. But he began to find a question in his mind, "Can it be that that British lieutenant was so poor an officer that he really had never thought about what is the best way for troops to load? Can it be that General Loudoun, like that other British general, Braddock, just doesn't know how to run a campaign against Indians? Can it be that the British Army really isn't as good as they think they are?"

September passed. The woods turned scarlet and gold in October. The bands of prowling French and Indians could see further, could send in their deadly bullets straighter than ever. Dysentery in camp stopped. The men, weakened by long sickness, began to die of pneumonia.

October was over. November weather, cold, dark, rainy, set in. The trodden-down ground around the fort was a sea of mud. The soldiers had only their summer foot-gear. Were they to stay there all winter?

Lieutenant Revere, silently doing his best to keep his sick, idle and disheartened men in order, had little to do in the evenings. He did not, like the British, fill this time up with drinking and playing cards. He often sat, for an hour or so, on a stump in front of his tent before he turned in for the night, and just thought. He went over and over in his mind everything he had seen and heard that summer, the first time he had lived close to Englishmen. An idea kept coming to him, an idea which was very astonishing to him. He thought, "Why, I don't like the British! We none of us do. We just don't like them."

December grew near. Snow began to fall. Drifts piled around tents.

Finally, on the 25th of November, a messenger came in from British headquarters. He brought at last the order to move. Not forward. They were to break camp and go home to Boston. Without having done a single useful thing since May, what Massachusetts men were still alive were to crawl back to Boston with the artillery that had never been fired.

Lieutenant Revere took an active part in packing up and starting the march back. Around him was a great deal of cursing, for everybody's nerves were frazzled to rags by that dismal summer. But he was silent. He was thinking.

He could hardly have told what he was thinking. His mind was in a tumble of troubled confusion. But somewhere, deep and dim, was another half-guessed-at idea. It was even newer and more astonishing to him than the other things he had been thinking. He couldn't stop to get it clear, because there was so much work to be done before leaving camp for the march home. He just caught pieces of this new notion—: "My father was French. But I'm not. My Hitchbourn grandfather was a British subject. But maybe——"

The thin, ragged soldiers stood in line. He gave the command, "Forward, *march*." But what he was thinking was, "If I don't have to be French, just because my father was, maybe I don't have to be British, because my grandfather was." He snapped out a command, "Close up the ranks!" But in his mind was a question he didn't know any answer to, "But if we weren't British subjects, what *would* we be?"

He was shocked to have had such an idea, and shoved his confused, wondering thoughts down out of sight.

Going Home

8

ALL along the slogging tramp home, he heard people
talking as though they too had, in the back of their
minds, the same kind of ideas. This time no flags flew
from the homes of the Massachusetts people at the
sight of the weary militiamen plodding in the snow beside pack horses loaded with ammunition that hadn't
been used. The farmers and village folks put on their

winter coats and caps and went out to speak kindly to
their own men. But the talk was not cheerful.

The militia soldiers told the Massachusetts people
just what had been happening—and put in all the trimmings, largely swear-words, I imagine. Paul was surprised to see that what they said about the British was
not new to these merchants, farmers and mechanics.
Many of the older men who listened to the angry story
of the young soldiers wagged their heads and said, "We
could have told you! We've served with them, too."

Over and over, the middle-aged farmers or blacksmiths asked, "How much good did your shined-up buttons do you, when an Injun from behind a tree . . ."
an imaginary musket was aimed, an imaginary trigger
pulled, "bang! bang! and down you went, no matter
how well you had brushed your hair." Paul nodded
glumly. Yes, it had been like that.

But the fur really flew, when these home people
along the march asked, *"What* did you think of the
English *officers?"*

When the American militiamen got started on what
they thought of the British officers, they shouted and
clenched their fists.

"The British officers just laugh at anybody who ex-
pects them to pay what they owe—except their gam-
bling debts."

"The British drink themselves sick like the Indians."

"The British look down on anybody who earns an
honest living."

"The one idea every rich Englishman has is to get a Government job with big pay and no work."

"They treat their privates like dogs. I'd knock down a man who treated a dog that way."

"The British . . . the British . . . "

Not only in Massachusetts, but all over the American colonies, the roads were filled with angry militiamen going home to spread the news of what "the British" were like. And everywhere, in villages, and on farms, they found fellow-Americans who agreed with them, having seen the same sort of thing when they were younger and serving in the militia.

Yet there were, it is true, some who didn't agree at all, who exclaimed, "Now hold on! You're talking about the Regular Army! Don't take them for the British nation! It's not the same thing. Thousands and thousands of English people at home aren't a bit like them red-coats."

Sometimes a man who had only recently come to the colonies said earnestly, "Why, from the first day I got to Massachusetts, I felt as though I had cousins all around me. English folks are just like anybody else. The people where I come from in Somersetshire have just the same ideas as you, about the decent way to act. I wasn't brought up to drink or gamble. My folks always pay their debts. I hardly even ever *saw* an Army officer till I came here. And my family's as British as British."

Mostly the grumbling American militia didn't pay much attention to such talk. To them it was just talk.

The officers in Albany who had been so disagreeable, the privates who had been so dumb—they had actually seen them.

Once Lieutenant Revere did answer back to a young farmer who was defending the ordinary people of England. He put a question sharply: "Why don't we see any of that kind of decent Englishmen you're talking about, in the Regular Army?"

"Why, man alive! To join up with the army is the last thing any honest, self-respecting, hard-working man in England would do. I was brought up to think that the only fellows who take up with military service are the no-goods. When we hear about a lad we know joining up with the army, we think it was because he didn't want to earn his own living. Or else he'd got into trouble and wanted to leave home before it was found out."

For nearly a hundred years before our Revolution, the soldiers and officers in the British Regular Army were almost the only English people seen in America by ordinary Colonials. So it was a poor report about "the British" which the militia returning from that summer's campaign spread all along the cold dreary march to Boston. It was a pity.

PART III

Some Education For an American

Inside the Revere Home, Daytimes

9

WHEN Paul Revere stepped back into his shop, his
own shop, every tool in it looked like an old friend.
When he shut his door—how blessèd it seemed to be
able to shut his door on what he had been through!—he
shut his mouth, too, on those six months. Like many—
like most—young men come back from war, he did not
want to talk about it. It had been bad enough to live
through it once, without telling it all over again.

And, like many—like most—families of young men returned home from the war, the Reveres knew from the minute they saw Paul that something serious had happened to him. It was not just that he was thinner than he ever had been, or that he was tanned and weather-beaten. No, he had changed into somebody else, like many a man who has been a soldier. They soon learned, as such families do, not to ask questions, not to try to find out what the matter was, just to go along from day to day, with what had to be done.

There was, fortunately for Paul, plenty of that. Mrs. Revere and Thomas had done their best to keep the business going, but Paul's first look at the bench and at the account books showed him that he was much needed. How good it seemed to close his strong hand around the handle of a hammer! His work took hold of him and filled his mind. He flung himself with all his might back into being himself. He was no longer Lieutenant Revere in uniform, he was plain Paul Revere, silversmith, artisan, in his shirtsleeves at a bench, a man who earned his living at a trade—and it felt fine!

Late in December 1756 was the date of the return of the long line of soldiers who had, like those in the nursery rhyme, marched up the hill and then marched down again. When January 1757 came in, Paul was twenty-two years old, a master silversmith, and one of the very best in America. He depended on nobody—on nothing but his own good head-piece and clever hands. He did not need to take orders from an officer above him in rank, and he did not need to give orders to men below him in rank. How he did like to live without looking up to, or down on, anybody! He could do what he pleased, so long as he paid his debts and was decently kind to his folks.

People married early in those days. Paul wanted to have a regular home life, and a family of his own as well as a much-loved shop and workbench. It wasn't long before Paul was married, to a girl who went to the same Church he did—for Paul went right on, always being a member of the Church his father had given up so much to belong to.

He couldn't see what he could *do* about the black question which had so troubled him out there in the harsh North Woods. Like a sensible man, he decided he would do nothing about it—for the time being. What he could do was to work hard and make a good living for his mother, his wife, his little sisters. That he did with all his heart. For his children also—the family-of-his-own came right along after his marriage, and the little home was soon bursting at the seams. Paul was always a good son, so he knew how to be a good father.

He took loving care of his little boys and girls, when they were well and when they were sick. Here's a story about that. One of the Revere children came down with small-pox. In those days people were frightfully afraid of this disease. Anybody who had small-pox was sent to a "pest-house," a dreadful place, where they stayed till they got well, or died. Mostly they died. But when the Boston officials came around to take the Revere child off to the pest-house, the upstanding young silversmith said, "No such thing." He'd take care of him at home, he said. They told him if he did, the whole family would have to be quarantined. His shop would be shut up and watched to make sure no customers came in or out. Paul Revere said he'd do whatever was legal. But he would not send a sick child of his out of his care.

For a whole month the Revere family were shut up in their small house. Mrs. Revere wasn't at all well. Paul and his old mother did most of the housework, nursing and amusing the convalescent children. Not one Revere died, young or old. The young father brought them all through.

He lost a lot of money that month, of course, by not taking on any orders for silversmithing. But he soon made that up, for he was a great success at his trade. He grew better and better at it. People gave him spendid orders for all kinds of important things. Not just shoe-buckles and silver thimbles, but big pieces of silverware, great bowls and cups, and finely shaped, beautifully decorated sugar bowls and cream pitchers and teapots. Business was good in Boston, trade by sea with all kinds of far-away places was flourishing, people had money to spare—and no banks to put it in. Lots of customers came to the Revere shop to place orders for platters and punch bowls. Paul now had a son, Paul, and it was understood that he would follow his father and grandfather. As soon as he was old enough, he would be apprenticed to this fine trade, which was also an art, of working in silver.

Outside the Revere House, Evenings

10

DID Paul forget about the long months when he had been a lieutenant in the American Militia? No, nobody can forget such things. He remembered every minute of those days as he worked hard at his bench and kept his eyes and ears open to what was going on around him. And now he began to realize that what was going on around him was history.

But history, even when you know you are living it, is

something like a football scrimmage. If you are out on the field in the line, all you can be sure about is what happens to the players close beside or in front of you. For that matter, people on the side lines often fool themselves in guessing where the ball will be when the whistle blows.

A football scrimmage takes only a minute or two. A history scrimmage sometimes takes ten years or longer before anyone can be sure which side has made an advance. For more than twelve years after Paul's return from being a soldier, Boston was the field for a long, long history-tussle. He was right in the middle of it too, for all he kept steadily at his tap-tap-tapping on his little anvil, making beautiful pieces of silverware.

He couldn't stop working, for he had the family living to earn. Yet he got into politics, up to his neck. This is how he managed to do it:—Boston people were gathering together in those days, in all kinds of clubs and societies and associations. At least those did who felt that the political rights of the American colonies were in danger from the British government. There were all kinds of organizations and Paul joined as many as he had time for. One was the orderly, serious old society of the Masons. Paul became a Mason. Another was as different as could be—a brand-new gang called "the Sons of Liberty." Paul became a Son of Liberty. There were others called "Caucuses." Another one was called "The Long Room Club." And there were others we don't know much about because they managed to keep their meetings secret. Paul Revere belonged to so many of these societies that he could go out nearly every evening to a meeting.

What did they do, for twelve years and more, at those long evening meetings? They talked.

Paul, like other returned soldiers, had kept his mouth grimly shut at home. You can't talk about life in the army to folks who haven't been there. But the men in these societies *had* been there. Most of them had served in one or another of the many campaigns against the French in Canada. Like Paul they had lived with the British Regular Army, they had taken orders from British officers. They put their heads together to com- pare notes on what they thought of the British (they really meant the British Regular Army) and found they all had the same ideas. The angry talk that had been bottled came out now in a long, hot rush.

It did them good to be in the midst of people who understood. You see, you can't rub out something that has happened just by not talking about it. It sticks in your memory, like a thorn. To talk it over with other people who have been through the same sort of thing is like getting a thorn out of your flesh.

So first of all, these evening meetings were full of talk about the smart-aleck, younger British officers who put on such airs and had, the Americans thought, so little to put on airs about. This kind of talk was full of anger. It had been piling up for years and years, while the British government kept sending to the colonies

just the kind of men to give Americans the idea that
they couldn't possibly get along with the English
people.

There were two reasons why many of the younger
British officers rubbed the Americans so furiously the
wrong way. At that time in English history, the only
kind of young men who were ever made officers were
from families with lots of property. And at that time
in England, children who grew up in families with
property were taught as a matter of course to look
down on people who worked for their livings. They
took for granted that they would be admired and looked
up to for not working.

But in the colonies it was just the other way around.
Mostly the people who didn't do something to make a
living were the shiftless and lazy. They were the ones
who were looked down on.

When the British army people, brought up with one
kind of idea, had to try to live with the American Colonials brought up with exactly the opposite idea, the
sparks flew. They couldn't do a thing together without
both sides getting angry.

That was one reason. The other reason was that the
younger British officers who were sent to the American
colonies were not by any means the finest in the British Army. To fight in a European war where the officers
of the other nations you met were also lords and dukes
and earls seemed much more worthwhile to British
gentry than fighting in North America. There, as like as

not, a young British lieutenant, although son of a lord, might have to associate with a Colonial who was a common working man. It was very annoying for a young British aristocrat to have an ordinary person like a silversmith think he had the right to ask him a question about the best way to have his men load their muskets, just as if he were the Britisher's equal. Who did he think he was—a *real* officer?

This was not true about all the higher officers. To be a general was worth anybody's while, even an earl's—even in America. So the high-up British officers were often very fine men, intelligent and understanding. But everyday Americans like Paul Revere and his hardworking friends in shops, on farms, on fishing sloops, making rope and barrels and shoeing horses—what chance did they have to know generals?

So with the most promising regimental officers doing their fighting in France or Germany, the British lieutenants and captains sent out with the troops to America were—not all, but many of them—like problem children in a class at school. Nobody liked them. Nobody knew what to do with them. Nobody wanted them around. It was a relief to the folks at home to get them packed off across the Atlantic where, for a while, their bad manners and bad habits wouldn't bother their families in England.

Now, nearly two hundred years later, we know all these things. But the ordinary Americans of Paul Revere's time hadn't the least idea of them. They took for granted—why wouldn't they?—that the whole British nation was like the British officers they detested.

Of course there are always many more private soldiers in any army than officers. Of the British private Regulars, there were two kinds: men who felt at home in the British military life and those who didn't. Those who didn't, found it fairly easy to walk away from barracks some dark night and vanish into the American farming land. The British officers always had their work cut out trying to locate their deserters. The others, the real Regulars who had been trained to be nothing but soldiers, were as proud of not working at a trade for their living as their officers were of not being in business. So they didn't add to the popularity of "the British" with Massachusetts people.

But of course personal dislike isn't enough to start a revolution. There were other things talked about in Paul Revere's evening "meetings," another kind of discussion, not loud and angry, but very intent and serious. This was about the law they all lived under. Paul Revere listened to this even more closely than to the angry kind, for he could learn something from it and he was one who always liked to learn.

In general, Massachusetts men had a better education than the same kind of men in England. English travelers who visited the colonies often wrote home about their surprise that so many perfectly ordinary people could read and write and keep accurate accounts of their money. The visitors were even more surprised that all Colonials—"even the women," they wrote—were interested in their government.

What these English travelers didn't think about—probably didn't know about—was the Town Meeting habit. In Massachusetts, all over New England, the plain, ordinary people like country blacksmiths, and tavern-keepers, and farmers, and city artisans voted at Town Meeting. And nearly everybody took his turn at being elected to some town office. They were used to being citizens, responsible, every man of them. They had ideas about how a country should be governed because they had ever so much more practice at making government work in their towns and villages than people like them in England of that day.

One thing they were sure of: that the only fair kind of government is based on law—not on what any one person wants to do. And the man who was the English king at that time paid less attention to the law and wanted his own way, law or no law, more than any English king has since. The Massachusetts people, not only the lawyers, everybody, kept their eyes closely fixed on him—George the Third, his name was—to make sure he did not try to push them around more than the English law allowed. A lot of those evening meetings were taken up with long careful study of what the law was. These plain men who studied the law and followed so closely every move the King and his Ministers and the English Parliament made, were like people watching a basketball game when they suspect the referee is giving one team all the best of it in calling fouls. They sat on the edge of their seats and never looked away from the trampling rush out on the floor. They wanted to be ready to jump to their feet and yell, *"No, you don't"* if the King or his Ministers or Parliament went too far.

Both Sides Get Their Backs Up

11

AMERICAN history was as much a part of Paul Revere's daily life as baseball is of yours. You can't get the hang of what he was up to, during those years when he was getting married and having a family, unless you know something about what was going on in his country.

There were two parts to what was going on. One

part was made up of facts. The other part was feeling, deep and hot.

Anybody could see the two principal facts: the first was that, only a few years after that forlorn nitwit performance in the North Woods, the British did put on a splendid well-planned campaign with fine energetic generals in charge, did defeat the French, did put the French government entirely out of Canada. The other plain fact was that the long wars against the French in Canada had cost a lot and had to be paid for. Where was the money coming from? The British said the wars had been carried on just to take care of the colonists. So the colonists ought to pay the bill. To this day the English think we didn't play fair on this point.

But the Americans knew that they had already spent a great deal in those wars. They had raised militia troops, many more in proportion to the number of colonists than the British had provided. They had paid these soldiers, and had voted the money for their food, clothing, care in sickness and other expenses. They also knew that many Englishmen had made enormous fortunes out of those wars, and they saw what everybody saw, that the British Empire had won millions of new acres. Why should they pay for those?

Moreover, the American taxpayers didn't enjoy the idea of raising money to pay for some of the going-ons of those fine British officers they didn't like. Part of the plan of the English government was to bring over some regular red-coated British troops to "protect" the American colonists. Protect them from whom, from what, the Americans wondered, now that there were no more French troops in Canada to bring down Indians in raids? And you can guess whether they enjoyed the notion of having more "regulars" around, and paying for them, into the bargain.

Still, everybody was thankful not to have any more French and Indian raids. They knew you don't get something for nothing. Sure, they would pay their share of what the wars had cost.

But how? That was the question. The only way a government can get money is by taxes. No hollow tree with gold in it, anywhere. The only place a government can find money is in people's pockets. But if the tax-money was coming out of American pockets, the Americans wanted some say-so about how much it was to be, and what kind of taxes were going to produce it.

Here we come to the deep feeling which, more than an ordinary quarrel about money, was at the bottom of the row with England. The feeling was that nobody should be made to live under rules he hadn't had any chance to vote for or against.

You remember the rules Paul Revere's gang of boys made for their "society?" Everybody in that club was to have just as much chance as anybody else to decide how the club was to be run. Those Boston boys didn't make that idea up out of their heads. They were ordinary boys. They only did what they had been brought up to do. They had never even heard of any other way to manage a group of people working together. Their club would have blown up with a bang if they'd tried any other way. But they never dreamed of any other way.

Well, the American fathers and mothers and grandparents who taught their boys that idea didn't invent it, either. The first settlers had brought it from England. In a sort of way, that idea was the foundation of English law. But English law was not clearly written out or understood. Some English people had a share in deciding how they should be governed. But thousands of Englishmen had no such share, and both the King and the party which was on top in English politics at this time were dead set against letting any more people vote, even right home in England, let alone thousands of miles off in the colonies.

It wasn't only George the Third. The French King, the Austrian Emperor and all the little kings and dukes in Germany held on tight to all the power they could get. Yet all the while the belief was growing—not only in England, but strongly in France and even a little in other parts of Europe—that Government must not be a one-man job with all the orders coming down from the top. In country after country this idea was boiling, while the rulers sat on the lid of the teakettle until it blew off.

But right now, in our story, it was in Boston that the steam pressure was highest.

There, men like Paul Revere hadn't any doubts. They had grown up with the idea that everybody should have something to say about the rules of his group. If the British Parliament was going to raise

money by taxes in the colonies, of course the colonists
should vote about them. The only way they could vote
was through men they had elected in America and sent
to the English Parliament in London. This seemed natural to the Boston Sons of Liberty.

But it did not seem perfectly natural, not by a long
shot, to the British King and his friends. They hadn't
the least idea of allowing even the people in England,
all of them, to have a fair representation in Parliament.

So the Parliament went ahead and voted the Stamp
Act to raise that money by taxes about which the
Americans hadn't had any say. The Americans blew up
with a bang. Especially the Boston people, who had a
special way of their own to make bangs, and noisy
ones.

They had learned, in those Guy Fawkes' day goings-
on, that by blacking up their faces and looking tough
and yelling and hammering on bells and drums as they
raced through the streets at night, they could scare the
rich people into staying indoors. They'd try some Guy-
Fawkesing on the British officials and their families.
It was the only way they had to make the British government realize that they did not intend to pay taxes
they hadn't voted on.

While the Sons of Liberty were making a big noise
in Boston streets, people all over America were refusing
to pay those taxes. After a while the British Parliament
tried new tactics. They rubbed out the Stamp Act. Just
withdrew it.

You can't imagine how excited and relieved the

Americans were about this news. They thought that their principle had won. They thought it meant the British agreed with them that nobody should pay taxes he had not voted on. Their hearts almost burst, they were so happy.

The day the ship came into Boston Harbor with the news that the Stamp Act was no more, the Boston people got up just the opposite kind of parade from the yelling, heavy-footed marching of the Sons of Liberty. People went along the street, playing sweet gentle music in front of Boston houses. The big tree on the Common, which they had come to call "The Liberty Tree," where the Sons of Liberty used to gather, was covered from bottom to top with bright-colored decorations. When darkness came every window in every Boston house had a lighted candle gleaming cheerfully in it.

Paul Revere and his wife and children joined the crowds of their neighbors, all carrying lighted lanterns. They gathered to stand, rejoicing, under the Liberty Tree, which was hung all over with lighted lanterns. They thought the danger of war with England was over. They thought the spirit of the English law had won out. And they loved that spirit. Everything was all right now.

But they were mistaken. The British King did not love the spirit of the English law. He hated it. And by this time he was pretty much the boss of the English government. He wanted to run things his way, law or no law. A great many British people didn't like this.

And the fact that a century before, they had pushed one English king off the throne, and cut off another king's head, showed that when their backs were up, they wouldn't take too many orders from anybody. But just at this time those who were against the King were not, like the Americans, their cousins, sitting on the edge of their seats, ready to jump up and yell "No you don't" if the King went beyond the law. All but a few of them seemed to be, for a while, like discouraged people who sag back and say, "Oh, what's the use."

The Americans didn't sag back. The King and his friends showed that they still thought they had the right to tax people as they liked, by voting another kind of tax on the colonies. The Boston people went back to their scary, noisy street-marching with blackened faces. They made themselves very disagreeable and alarming. (As a matter of fact, since sober, level-headed men like Paul Revere always went out with them to make sure they didn't go too far, they did not, in those years, do any serious harm.) British officials sent back word to England that they needed some regular soldiers to put down these screeching Boston crowds.

So the next move, in the long swaying to and fro of the struggle between the two sides, was that the British government did send some regular soldiers to Boston.

The very sight of their red uniforms brought hated memories to men like Paul Revere. And there were many like him. Only a few Americans who had money enough to live in style, and so were not looked down on by the British officers, were glad to see them come. Everybody else stood silent on the Boston streets, looking sourly at the British regiments that landed on the wharf. Dressed in their best uniforms, the soldiers marched into town, keeping step perfectly to the drum and fife corps, every knee bent at the same instant, every foot hitting the ground, *thump!* at the same time. Men like Paul Revere were not impressed. They had seen that before.

The "Regulars" were about as comfortable with the Boston men, women and children as the American militia had been in the North Woods with the mosquitoes, black-flies and ticks. Every day, all day long, they were bothered and pestered. Boston men would "accidentally" shove a British redcoat off the wharf into the sea, and be out of sight when the soldier climbed back, dripping. Boston women yelled bloody murder if any English soldier said so much as "Good morning" to them. But the little boys, like the gnats, were almost the worst.

They were harder to catch than grownups. They put two fingers in their mouths and whistled, forty or fifty of them together. They threw snowballs, and sometimes put stones into the balls. A bunch of them would gather around a British sentry, splendid in his red uniform, the straps and trimmings as white as his thickly powdered hair. One of the boys would step out in front of the gang, and yell at the sentry:

"Lobster back! Lobster back!
You're going to lose your claws,"

and then scurry back to the gang. The soldier looked like a giant compared to the boys, but there wasn't much he could do. He'd pull his big cocked hat down on his head and take long steps out toward the boys, his fists doubled up, shouting, "Which of ye said that?"

The boys would burst out laughing and yell, "Ye-e-eah! Don't you wish you knew," and scatter in all directions.

No sentry is allowed to go far from where he is posted. This one could only go back there and stand grumbling, hearing the boys hooting and catcalling from the alleyways.

Both sides had their backs up. The British would not let Americans send elected men of their own to the British Parliament to help decide about the taxes. The Americans would not pay those taxes till they did.

In all the countries in those days which had "well-disciplined" regular armies, the soldiers fought bravely and well on a battlefield. But between battles, when they settled down for a while where they could see the people around them living without "iron discipline," they naturally began to desert. Over in Austria about this time, a "disciplined" army lost about a quarter of its soldiers from desertion. The British regiments in Boston were made up of English-speaking men who could understand what was going on around them in the colonies. A good many of them liked the looks of it.

They began to melt away into the Massachusetts countryside to settle down and become Americans. From the stream of these deserters who settled among them, the Americans heard a lot about the British Army as seen from the inside. It sounded as bad as they had thought, and didn't make them like "the British" any better than before.

All this time—twelve years or so—Paul Revere, making beautiful pieces of fine silverware, earning a good living for his family, was, by day, a good family man. Nearly every evening he went out to one or another of his clubs and listened to the talk of men who had had much more book-education than he ever had. Like them, he was thinking and thinking, trying to make sense out of what was happening.

Lots was happening. The British tried a different kind of taxes. The Americans refused to buy anything from England. This meant a big money loss to businessmen in England, for whom the colonies were a fine market. And anyhow, a good many of them already thought the King was going too far. The Lord Mayor of London put on the dress-up clothes he had to wear to speak to the King and went with a lot of the Aldermen of London (also dressed in the proper clothes) to tell the King that they didn't like the way the English government was treating the Americans, and they wished the King would stop it. The King was furious to have ordinary people, not lords or dukes, speak their minds to him. He said he never again would receive the Mayor and Aldermen. So that was that.

Over in Boston, a silversmith working away in his shirt-sleeves began to hear, as if in his ear, the answer to that question which had so shocked him when he first thought of it in the North Woods—"If I'm not French and not British, what is there I can be?"

He knew now what he could be. He could be something nobody had heard of till then. He could be an American.

He never made speeches, Paul Revere didn't. He never made a speech about being an American. But from this time on, he acted like an American with all his heart.

And very soon, a chance to act came his way. After a while the British made another play in the long match they were having with the Americans. They took off every single tax. Except one. One small tax on one small item of no importance. Tea.

Most people in Boston, elsewhere in Massachusetts, and other places in America were worn out by the long scrimmage. The British guess was that the colonies couldn't get up enough energy to make a fuss over one measly little tax of a few cents a pound. They guessed wrong.

PART IV

King George Gets
Very Angry

Several New Things in the Revere Home

12

IN 1773, the Revere children had a new mother. Their own mother fell ill and died, leaving all that big family without anybody to take care of them except Paul's mother. But she was too old to take care of a lot of children for long. And Paul was too young to live alone all the rest of his life. He married again, and very well too. A fine, kind-hearted, vigorous, sensible Boston young woman, who had a mind of her own and was a great comfort to the young father and his children. They soon loved her and depended on her, and she stood by them all the rest of her long life.

Through her, the Reveres came to know a person quite new to them. This was an old woman, a relative of the new Mrs. Revere. Well, sort of a relative. An in-law. She was married to an old cousin of Rachel Revere. He had been a sailor in his youth, and on one of his trips to England had met the lively, good-looking Barbara Weston, had married her and brought her back to Boston. So she was as English as anybody could be.

Yet she did not have a single idea like those the Reveres had thought all people in England had. Aunt Barbara spoke English in a rough, rolling sort of way unlike their own Boston talk. But except for that, she agreed exactly with the Reveres about how to manage life. She had no more patience than they had for fine gentlemen in fine clothes who never worked for their livings. She was as disgusted as any Boston person by the way the British officers gambled, didn't pay shopkeepers for what they bought, and got drunk. She was as shocked as anybody else about the frightful floggings the private soldiers got for doing anything their officers had said not to. Time and again she helped soldiers to escape from the British Army and slip off into the farming country of Massachusetts to become Americans.

She hated the very word "Regular" as much as any American did. Like them she hated the idea back of it, of men who never, all their lives long, learned to do anything except to fight, and in between fights, to march around, shine their buttons, and remember to do exactly as they were told. She spoke out as roughly as any of the people in Paul's evening clubs about not giving in to the King about those taxes unless they had a fair chance to vote on them. But there was one point of disagreement. She insisted that the Regular Army sent over to keep Boston down wasn't in any way like the big bulk of British people back home. Paul had heard that once or twice before, but he needed reminding to keep from forgetting it—and it was an entirely new idea to his children.

Old Aunt Barb often came in to visit Mrs. Revere. There was always a great deal of housework to do so she pitched in and helped out, for all she was little and old and bent over with rheumatism. But no matter whether she was rocking a baby to sleep, or washing dishes or peeling potatoes, she stopped short to scold any Revere—Paul himself, too—who spoke, as so many plain workingmen and women in Boston did, about their dislike for "the British."

"Don't talk like a fool," she would say, shaking out a dishcloth as she hung it up, or stuffing a pillow into its case. "There are just as many kinds of British as there are Americans, make no mistake about *that*. The folk where I was brought up, in Manchester, the people in Birmingham—they would fit right into this home or any other in Boston where people are earning their own livings, and you'd never know the difference. I wasn't taught to look up to worthless fine folks any more than you. We don't take off our hats and bow our heads to them either. They're not the only kind of people in England, make no mistake about *that*."

Sometimes behind her back, the Revere children called her "Aunt Make-no-Mistake."

Something else happened that year of 1773—the Reveres owned a horse. All of a sudden in the records of their family, a horse of their own appeared. A barn was run up to shelter this animal. Paul Revere's neighbors knew him as a hard-working silversmith who hardly ever stepped out of his shop by day and had no reason to go away from Boston streets at any time. They may have wondered what in the world did he want of a horse?

It is almost funny, isn't it, that we, nearly a hundred and eighty years after that horse was led into the new barn, can guess much better than Paul Revere's next-door neighbors did, in 1773, why just at that time, the silversmith took to riding horseback.

Yet it wasn't long before they knew, too. The Revere horse had been in and out of that barn only about long enough to give the city-bred Revere children time to get used to it, and to learn how to feed it apples, when Paul Revere began to ride off on it for long, hard trips. Those jolting rides in summer, over the rough, rutted, muddy roads in winter, through blizzards, over ice and snow, had a good deal to do with his coming to be that brand-new kind of person, an American. And with our being Americans, too.

In those days a ship or a horse was the only way of getting word to one place of what had been going on in another place. Ships were sailing-vessels, and they depended entirely on the wind. If there wasn't enough wind, they were stuck fast where they were. If there was too much wind, they were blown far away from where they wanted to go. A man on horseback could keep going no matter what the weather was. Especially if the man was Paul Revere, carrying important news.

The news from Boston was certainly important that year of 1773. It was so exciting that Boston has never forgotten it, nor has any other place in the U.S.A. It was the start of a change in our life so tremendous that no American boy or girl ever gets through the eighth grade of any school in our country without learning about it.

The doings began, late in November, when an English ship sailed into Boston harbor and tied up at a Boston wharf, just like hundreds and hundreds of other ships. But this was different from any other. Its cargo was tea. The price was low. But everybody who bought a pound of it would be paying a tax that he hadn't had a chance to vote on. All those Massachusetts and New England people had grown up in the habit of everybody's having a chance to show by his vote what he thought about the rules he lived under. They were used to that idea, all right. But would they stand up for the idea on such a little thing as a few cents extra price for every pound of tea they bought? Would they think it worthwhile?

Yes, they did. The loudest and most up-and-doing of the clubs and caucuses Paul Revere belonged to— the Sons of Liberty—put posters all over the city to invite Boston people to a big mass-meeting. The crowd at that meeting voted to tell the owner of the tea-ship not to unload that tea. They warned him to leave it right where it was, locked in big chests, deep down inside the ship.

By this time the officials of Boston (they were appointed from England, so of course they were on the British side) had been disturbed and bothered and scared by the slam-bang noisiness of the thousands and thousands of Boston men and big boys who marched around the streets at night, carrying torches, and shouting that Americans would not pay the taxes they had not voted on. The officials and their soldiers, too, moved again out to Castle Island in the harbor where there were British cannon to fire on anybody who might try to get near them to yell any slogans about votes and taxes.

The Sons of Liberty had no legal right to give orders to anybody. But with all the British officials and soldiers out of Boston, there weren't any guards around who might have protected the shipowner if he had tried to unload his cargo. In fact there were guards around to make sure that he didn't. Twenty-five Sons of Liberty, armed like soldiers, marched up and down the wharf all through that November night, watching the ship. Not a pound, not an ounce, not a leaf of that tea was to be taken into Boston.

Was Paul Revere, the silversmith, one of this armed guard? What do you think? Of course he was.

Everybody knew that there was one thing the ship-owner might do. He might sail out of the port of Boston and go to some other harbor—there were plenty of them nearby like Salem or Portsmouth—get his tea-chests up from the hold of his ship, out on the dock, and into a warehouse. Then he could start back to England in a hurry and get out of this hornet's nest buzzing around his ears. But the Sons of Liberty didn't want it unloaded anywhere in North America. So the next day after they had kept a watch on the dock, six of them were sent out—on horseback of course—to warn the people in port-towns where there were wharves.

Was Paul Revere one of the six? What's your guess? Of course he was. That new horse was saddled and bridled; Paul Revere's children saw their father pull on his riding-boots, and get into his warm outdoor riding clothes.

"Here's your cap, Father."

"Let me get you your other muffler. It's warmer."

"Oh Father, let *me* buckle on your spurs! I've practiced lots. I know just how to."

"Shall I put up a lunch for you, Paul?"

No, this first ride with important news wouldn't be a very long one—only to a nearby town. He'd get something to eat when he got there.

"Where did you put the letter you're going to take?"

Paul Revere tapped his forehead. "The news is inside here," he said. No enemy sentry could take it away from that hiding place.

Young Paul held the horse's head, very proud. Scared, too, as he thought of what would happen to them all if their father were put into prison for fighting back against the masters of the country. The Reveres hadn't a penny to pay for food and things to wear, except what their father earned day by day. And as Aunt Barb would have said, "Make no mistake," he got no money for his dangerous work for the Sons of Liberty, for his express-riding, for risking prison.

Young Paul looked at his kind, brave-hearted stepmother. She was smiling up at the horseman. If she was scared she didn't let anybody see it. Young Paul remembered what his father had told them so often about his French grandfather and stood firm.

His father said, "Goodbye, children. Be good. Goodbye, my dear girl."

He was off, soberly walking the horse down the narrow dark alley, and then trotting slowly down the street. He was nearly forty, and had too much sense for any galloping, show-off monkeyshines. He only had one horse. And he was going to need that horse for many other carrying-the-news rides.

The Ships Must Be Unloaded

13

THINGS got thicker along the Boston docks. Two more British ships sailed into the harbor and tied up beside the first one. They were loaded with chests of tea, too. The word began to go around that the tea on the three ships was worth a lot of money. Ninety thousand dollars' worth. That's a great sum even now. In those days it meant much more.

The question of what to do about it was like a riddle

that nobody knew the answer to. What the Sons of Liberty and everybody on their side wanted was to have those ships turn around and sail back to England with the tea-chests still down in their holds. Probably, seeing which way the wind blew in Boston, the owner of the ships wouldn't have liked anything better than to do just that.

But he couldn't, because of a Massachusetts law which required every ship to leave its cargo behind before it left port. This law allowed only twenty days to get the cargo out of the ship's holds. Because of the law the owner couldn't leave without unloading that expensive lot of tea. Because of the watch kept by the Sons of Liberty, he couldn't unload it. He probably bit his nails a good deal during those twenty days, trying to think of some way to untangle that knot.

There was one simple way to untie it. The Governor of Massachusetts could say he would allow an exception to the law in this case. The owner of the ships went to see the Governor to ask him to solve the riddle in this simple way.

But the Governor of Massachusetts was appointed by the British government, not elected by Massachusetts votes. You know which side he would be on in any quarrel. The British side, of course. So he said no. He not only said no, but he told the shipowner (and everybody else, too), that he had given orders to the British artillery out on Castle Island to fire on the ships if they tried to leave the harbor with those tea-chests still aboard.

The shipowner came back from the suburb of Boston where the Governor was, and gave this answer to the American colonists, on guard with loaded guns to keep that tea from coming in.

"There's nothing else I *can* do but unload my cargo. I must."

"No, you don't. You leave it right there. Not a pound of it is going to be sold here."

"Look, what do you *expect* me to do? I'm not in on this row. I don't own that tea! I'm just hired to carry it. But I do own the ships. And there won't be kindling-wood left of them if the cannon on Castle Island fire on them."

"You leave that tea where it is. You'll be fired on, all right, if you try to unload it."

All over Boston, people talked of nothing else. It had been November 28th when the first ship came in. Twenty days from that something would have to happen. People looked up the dates on their almanacs. Children counted them up on their fingers. One side or other of that tug-of-war would have to give way. Which?

People walked fast, talked fast, ate fast, didn't sleep very well at night. Aunt Barb's tongue flew as fast as anybody's. She kept breaking in on the talk. "Stick up for yourselves! There are plenty of folk across the water who wish you well. There's many and many an English city forty times as big as Boston," (she was stretching it a little) "that hasn't a man of its own in Parliament to speak up for it. My own Manchester's one. And Sheffield. And Leeds. And Birmingham. They all pay taxes they haven't any say-so about. And they don't like it any better than Boston does. Stand your ground here and they'll be freer men for it."

People in Boston had too much else to think about to pay much attention to a rheumatic old woman. What she said seemed to go in one ear and out the other. What was on their minds was a lot of tea that must never be sold in America.

The days went by, each one more exciting than the one before. When a tractor or a car is standing still with the engine running, you know what happens when somebody steps on the gas harder and harder, without letting in the clutch. The zooming of the engine gets louder and louder till the floor-boards shake. Boston was like that in those days.

When the legal time was almost up for the unloading of the chests of tea, the owner of the ships went out once more to see the British-appointed Governor. He would try again to persuade Governor Hutchinson to make just one exception to that law, and let him go back to England with his cargo unloaded. The tea-ship which had gone to Philadelphia had turned around and taken the tea back to England. Why couldn't *he?*

The Sons of Liberty called a meeting to hear what the shipowner said when he came back. It certainly turned out to be a mass meeting for fair! Seven thousand people went to it, more than half the number of men, women, and children in the city. All kinds of people hurried along the streets to Old South Church, the biggest building in Boston. Probably if you'd been in a Boston school that day, your teacher would have said, "Class dismissed for the day. Everybody in school over to the mass meeting." And you'd have trooped over there with the other students. Maybe you'd have all stood in the street outside, for there was then no building in America big enough to take in the crowd at that gathering.

But even if you and your teacher and classmates couldn't get inside the meeting, you'd have been in the thick of it. For inside the building and outside, everybody knew what he was waiting for. And they didn't wait around without saying anything. They'd have burst if they'd tried to, everybody was so excited. Speeches were made, lots of them, all that afternoon.

Outside in the street only a little of what went on inside could be heard, of course. But when the crowd inside the building cheered, or applauded, or groaned loudly, or jeered over something a speaker had said, those in the streets took it up, and did their own applauding and cheering and groaning. Then a hush would come inside, and they'd know that a new speaker had climbed up into the pulpit.

Whenever this happened, the thousands of waiting people out on the street said "Sh! Keep still!" and put their hands to their ears to listen.

Parts of sentences would come out of the open windows:

"The clouds are rising thick and fast on our American horizon . . ."

"Now is the time to save our country from tyranny . . ."

"The detested tea now in the harbor . . ."

"Every friend of our country, every man who wants his grandchildren to be free . . ."

The crowd hardly needed to hear what the speakers were saying. They knew it by heart, or they wouldn't have been there.

Pretty late in the afternoon, another kind of hush came. This time it started out in the street, and spread to the inside of the building. "Hush! Keep still. Sh!" The word went around in whispers, "The owner of the ships has come back from the Governor's house. There he is. Give him room to get by."

If you'd been one of the scholars dismissed from class to attend that meeting, you'd have held your breath now, you'd have pushed back against the crowd as hard as you could to make way for the shipowner. You'd have watched him climb up the steps to the church. You would have been careful not to make any noise, not even to scrape your shoe against the cobblestone paving. You wouldn't have coughed for anything, as along with those thousands of other people you stood silent, craning your neck to try to hear what the shipowner's report from the Governor was.

The Tea-Party

14

AS A matter of fact you wouldn't ever have heard what
he said. You wouldn't need to. A wild yell broke out.
You knew. The Governor had once more refused!

The big, solid old building seemed to rock. Men and
boys exploded through the doors and windows, their
faces flaming, shouting, "To the wharf!" "The Governor
says the ships must be unloaded. THEY WILL BE UN-
LOADED." And "Boston Harbor a teapot tonight."

There was a racing of feet down the dark streets, for this was in December and darkness begins early then.

Everybody ran as if he knew just where he was going. And so he did. The Sons of Liberty were as good at planning things beforehand as they were at torchlight marches in the streets. Everything had been settled. Each person knew just what he was to do if the Governor refused to let the ships go back to England with the tea.

What they did was to hurry to various places where they had, all ready to put on, those same crazy-looking duds they had often worn during Guy Fawkes Day processions.

They got into these in double-quick time. The rough old clothes were put on inside out. Their stocking-caps were pulled low down on their heads. They spread grease thickly on their faces as they always did, so the soot would stick. But that night they daubed on some smears of red paint as well. The idea was to dress up as Indians—sort of Indians. Their children had been out in the hen-houses to gather up what loose feathers they could find, and these were stuck every-which-way into their knit caps. The men didn't look much like Indians. But they didn't look much like what they were, either, serious-minded, hard-working Boston men.

Then they were off, in little groups of two or three, stepping resolutely down the cobbled streets that led to the wharf. Boys scampered at their heels, and were not told to go home. And if there was any child in

Boston who asked "What are those funny-looking men in queer clothes going to do? Mother, Mother, what are they going to do?" he must have been a very young child indeed.

Down at the wharf, the three ships lay silent and still. The "Indians" divided themselves into three groups, one for each ship, each squad under its own leader. They did not need to speak, more than to give the Indian grunts they used as part of their disguise. They knew just what they were to do. One thing they were not to do, and did not, was a single bit of damage to the ship or crew, or to steal as much as a teaspoon to take home with them.

They got aboard the ships, and told the mates to give them the keys of the storerooms and to get lanterns lighted. In no time, the big chests of tea were being hoisted up from the hold to the decks and the tops pried open.

British fighting ships with cannon were anchored on the water close to them. Every minute they expected to be attacked. They worked at top speed, breaking open the chests and shoveling the tea over the side of the ship, into the water. Ninety thousand dollars' worth!

They knew what would happen to every one of them, if they were caught.

Paul Revere knew that if he were tried for this, he would be in prison for years. He would lose his beloved silver-making shop, together with every penny he had, and his wife and children would have nothing to live on. Did this danger slow him up? No, faster and faster he scooped out the tea that might mean ruin for everything he loved, and shoveled it over the ship's railing into the salt sea.

At any moment he expected to have the guns from the British warships blast them off the decks in a murderous blaze. "Here, boy," he said, "take my turn with the shovel. They're slow getting those chests up. We'll never be done by dawn at this rate. I'll go help at the hoists."

On the docks, just on the other side of the ship's railings, stood a great crowd of Boston people. A good many of them had been yelling and shouting at that noisy mass meeting. Now, although there were thousands of them, they did not make one sound. As silent as though they were holding their breath, they stood watching ninety thousand dollars being thrown away —to defend an idea.

This was far too serious to yell about. They and their city might be ruined by this night's doings. But not one Boston voice was raised against it. They stood as still as statues watching those black-faced men and boys shoveling tea into the salt-water. Something was at last being done, not shouted about.

The clutch took hold; the engine that had roared while it was standing idle went into gear, the wheels made their very first turn; the American car began to move forward under its own power.

Dawn was showing in the east when the "Indians," the boys tagging at their heels, and the thousands of people on the wharf, got back to their homes. They had scarcely breath enough left to say to their families, "The ships are unloaded."

They wiped the grease and red paint from their faces, gave the rooster-feathers to the children to play with, shook the tea out of their shoes, took off their crazy-looking clothes and—most of them—fell into bed for a rest.

But not Paul Revere.

If the Americans were to stick together—not just the Massachusetts people, not just the New England people, but all the American colonies—the others in far-away cities like New York and Philadelphia must be told what had been done here in Boston.

Somebody must "ride express" (that meant at top speed) with a message from the Boston committee in charge of things. A lot of men were ready to go. But it took more than just young strength and endurance to make that long ride. At the end, the rider must show good judgment, must be a worthy representative of Boston, must, above all, know every single thing that had been happening, for he certainly would be cross-questioned and by very important people. You know without my telling you that Paul Revere was chosen to go.

"But, *Father*, aren't you too tired to start right off now?"

"Deborah, you know your father is never tired! Paul,

you'll need your saddlebags. How many clean shirts shall I put in for you?"

"Father, we boys can saddle and bridle the horse. Let us do it."

"Rachel, dear girl, put in some soap and my razor. And my old slippers. My feet'll be tired by night."

By the time the committee had finished writing the report on the night's doings, and had sent a hurried messenger with it to the Revere house, Paul was on his horse, the reins in his hands.

"Rachel, Paul, take care of the shop. Write down in the account book any money that comes in to pay for the silver-work. And if any orders come in, be sure to make a note exactly what size is wanted."

He was off again, broad-shouldered, middle-aged, vigorous, sober-faced, looking very much as your father would look if he were starting out for a long cold ride of 350 miles through mid-winter storms.

David and Goliath

15

YOU'VE probably seen the fire department go tearing by on the way to a three-alarm fire, bells ringing, whistles hooting, the big red fire engine and the hook-and-ladder trucks clattering down the street. The Boston Tea Party set off King George III into just such a "get-out-of-the-way" rush. With him, were those English people who agreed with him, and those who were afraid of him. He always went into a rage with any-

115

body who didn't agree with him, and he never forgave people, English or American, who showed they had minds of their own. The citizens of Massachusetts had showed, more openly than anybody else, that they did not agree with him and had minds of their own, so he now was in a fury against them.

Dislike always goes both ways; people dislike those who don't like them. Everyday Massachusetts people simply couldn't bear the kind of Britishers they met as army officers and British officials. It was only natural that this special kind of English people detested Massachusetts folks. Every idea one side had about the right way to run life seemed bad to the other side.

After the Boston Tea Party, those other English and Scots, plain folks and fine ones too, with very much the same ideas as Americans, had less chance than ever to stand up to the King. They were like people who happen to be on the streets when the fire-department trucks come screeching along, sweeping right through the traffic lights. Nobody can do much more than scramble up on the sidewalks out of the way. And yet, as old Aunt Barb reminded the Reveres, a great many of them did not believe for a minute that the Massachusetts people had set the English-speaking house on fire, when they wouldn't obey a command they thought was against the law. Such English people felt, and some of them said, that the Americans were only trying to keep the King from tearing down the law-abiding house that English-speaking people wanted to live in.

When King George felt like going his own way, even

against the legal traffic lights, he stepped hard on the gas, and kept his alarm gong banging so loudly it was hard for anybody to hear himself think. The members of the British Parliament at that time did not really represent the British nation. They were mostly of the King's kind anyhow. They, too, objected very much to every idea the Americans had. And even if they hadn't, a good many of them would have made believe they did, because they were afraid of the King. It was well known that if you agreed with King George III, you and your sons and your second cousins and your wife's folks got official jobs with big salaries, and no work at all to do. On the other hand, if you ever ventured to show that you didn't want him to have every single thing his own way, you and your family were apt to lose any government jobs you might have, even if you worked hard and honestly at them. With all his power —and he had a lot—the King punished people he didn't like.

Since he detested the Massachusetts people, he wanted to punish them so terribly that never again in England or in the colonies would anybody dare to go against him. He wanted to pick out just what the Massachusetts people loved most, and tear it up and trample it down.

What did the Massachusetts people love most? Their rights as free men to run their own government. Very well! He would see to it that Parliament passed laws to take away those rights. From now on it was not only in the sessions of the Sons of Liberty that Paul Revere heard long discussions about what was going on across the Atlantic. Nobody in Boston shops or offices talked of anything except the news brought by the latest ship about what was being said in London and done by Parliament. And since the news was no longer secret, Paul felt free to pass it on to his wife and children.

The Revere children no longer needed to be told to listen and try to understand politics, and not get so wrapped up in their play. It was like being in the midst of a terrific storm, with worse weather coming. What was being said in fierce, excited voices by their elders seemed much more exciting to the children than hide-and-seek. They hung around, their mouths open, and listened for dear life. When they could not understand the big words, they asked their older brother or their mother to explain afterwards.

"The port is to be closed." The children did not at first know why these simple words were said so that they sounded like a clap of thunder.

"Paul, what does it *mean*—'the port is to be closed'?"

Their big brother said hotly, "Don't you know *any-thing?* No ships, none at all, will be allowed to come in. If they try, the British cannon on Castle Island will blow them to smithereens. It means we won't have anything to eat except what little can be brought in by land. They're saying to us, 'You pay for that tea, or you'll all starve to death'."

"Well, will we pay for the tea?"

"We will *not*," said big brother. "If we pay, we'll be giving up to them that they have a right to make us pay any taxes they've a mind to get out of our hides."

"Well, will we starve to death?"

"We'll see about that." The big boy repeated a saying he often heard in his father's shop.

Two weeks later, a new wave of excited talk passed over Boston. The English Parliament had passed a law, forbidding Town Meeting—*Town Meeting*—except when the town begged the Governor for permission to have it.

Even the younger ones among those New England children knew what an awful, unthinkable idea it was, that a Town couldn't hold its annual Town Meeting to make the rules it was to live under for the next year. They didn't need to ask anybody why that sounded like a roll of thunder right over the house. But they did say, "Paul, the Governor's right here in Massachusetts. To ask him is not like asking the *King's* leave."

"Yes, it is too. We don't elect the Governor. The King appoints him. He's the King's man. He has to do what the King tells him to, or the King will kick him out."

"But suppose a Town did ask leave to have Town Meeting, and the Governor said 'all right, go ahead.' What'd be the matter with that?"

"What kind of a Town Meeting would it be, when you knew if you voted something the King didn't like, you wouldn't be allowed to meet again?"

Then a story was told around that the younger children couldn't make anything out of. One of the English lords said in public, in Parliament, that men without property who worked for their livings, like the Massachusetts farmers, shopkeepers, shipbuilders, carpenters, blacksmiths, had no business trying to run their own government.

"Why,—why—who *would* run their government?" asked the bewildered little Reveres, when they could get their older brother off to one side.

"Men trained to do nothing at all for their livings," he told them, "the kind of gentlemen we see in gold lace and scarlet broadcloth, playing cards all day long, and getting dead drunk at night."

"But Paul, that doesn't make sense!" those American children protested.

"I'll say it doesn't make sense," the big boy said shortly.

His father overheard this talk, and came down on the older brother sharply. "You are not *trying* to make the children understand," he said. "Now you take the time to tell them what it really does mean. You're not old enough to carry a musket, to ride express for your country. But you can do this—make your little brothers and sisters understand what's going on. They're American children. It's due them."

Aunt Barb was so old she sometimes scolded Paul as he scolded his son. One day he told a story that was going the rounds of Boston then, about a member of the English Parliament who had called the Massachusetts people "pernicious levelers," and said he had the proof of it from a letter a British friend had written him. Passing through Boston, the Englishman had called at a Massachusetts home. When the servant opened the door, the English visitor asked, "Is your master at home?" The servant answered, "My master? I have no master but Jesus Christ."

The little Reveres listened to the outburst of angry laughter from the grownups about this story, without getting any point to it at all. As soon as there was a pause, they asked their father, "What is 'pernicious'? What is a 'leveler'?"

Paul Revere had explained, " 'Pernicious' means all wrong. And a 'leveler' is a person who thinks that a man who works for his living is as good as an idler who doesn't."

"Well, of *course!*" cried the Boston children.

"Not a bit 'of course' in England," said Paul Revere. "There, a man who works is supposed to call his employer who doesn't work 'my master'."

Here Aunt Barb came sailing in. " 'In England! In England!' *Where* in England? Paul, you don't really try to make your children understand. You never give them any idea that all English people aren't like the King's men in London running the government now. Where I was brought up, in Manchester, and that is just as English as King George and more, too, people don't call their employer 'my master.' There are millions of that kind of English people."

"If they're so many," said Paul Revere, "why do they let the King get a law passed forbidding us to vote for the men on our own Council, so he can put his own men in? And how about our judges and juries now having to be appointed by the King?"

Aunt Barb was not to be put down. "My kind of Englishmen—and yours—just happen not to be on top in English politics now. But they're there—your own folks, who don't like the King's doings any better than you do."

But one time Aunt Barb, instead of scolding, was a comfort to the Reveres. One evening after supper, Paul and his wife were talking to each other, rather sadly. "If it comes to war, I wonder if we have a chance. Even one fighting chance," said Paul. "They have everything—a big regular army, who've been taught and taught to be soldiers. Everybody says nobody can stand up against the British Regulars in battle. And they've got all the money in the world. And all the gunpowder they want. And factories to make more. And all the big ships. And big cannon. And what have we? Some old squirrel guns our grandfathers left us. No money. Enough gunpowder for a few shots apiece. We don't know how to make any more. And if we did, where could we get the muskets?"

Aunt Barb was rocking the youngest baby to sleep. Over his little downy head she said, "First Samuel 17:40."

They turned around to her, surprised. She held out her hand. "Where's your Bible?" she said, and when they had given it to her, she read aloud:

"And David took his staff in his hand and chose him

five smooth stones out of the brook; and his sling was in his hand: and he drew near to Goliath.

"And when Goliath saw David, he disdained him, for he was but a youth.

"And Goliath said to David, 'I will give thy flesh unto the fowls of the air and to the beasts of the field.'

"Then said David to Goliath, 'Thou comest to me with a sword, and with a spear, and with a shield: but I come to thee in the name of the Lord of hosts.

" 'This day will the Lord deliver thee into mine hand; that all the earth may know that there is a God in Israel.

" 'And all this assembly shall know that the Lord saveth not with sword and spear.' "

Paul said, "Yes, this is a fight between soldiers—and men."

Aunt Barb laid the baby down in his cradle and said over her shoulder, "My Manchester folks are men, as much as you here—make no mistake about that. And they are praying that the men may win against the soldiers. You're standing up for their rights as well as your own."

PART V

The First Round of
The Big Fight

Boston Port Is Closed

16

BOSTON got the news that the harbor was to be closed on the tenth of May. Four days later a mass meeting was called. Right after that Paul Revere's fourteen-year-old son saddled and bridled his father's horse, and the express rider was off again to carry to New York and Philadelphia the news that Massachusetts was not going to take this lying down.

Twelve days later, when he came back to Boston

(how that man could cover ground on a horse!) he found that British General Gage had arrived to close the port. He had a lot of soldiers to back him up, enough so that there was now one British soldier for every two Boston people. In the harbor were British warships with loaded cannon on their decks. Now the British could shut out entirely the ships that brought in food. They thought they had a strangle-hold on Boston.

But from all over the country supplies came in by land. It was a regular show for the Revere children, city-bred as they were, to go down to the road over the Neck, and watch the stream of wagons trundling by, loaded with sacks of rice from South Carolina, with bags of wheat from Maryland, heaped up with salt codfish from nearby Marblehead, with rye and wheat flour from other Massachusetts towns. Sometimes there were whole droves of cattle brought in, under the care of weather-beaten countrymen in faded, well-washed smocks, or leather aprons, such as working-people wore then.

The children loitering around would look away from the procession of food carts and stare at the faces of the English army men. It was great fun. And how dumb of the British, the children thought, to keep ships out but let in anything that came by land . . . even cargoes unloaded at nearby harbors. They didn't understand that official orders said only to close the port. And in the British Army you had to follow orders and never use your own judgment about what was sensible. The youngsters didn't understand, either, how hard it is to feed a city with no more than can be hauled by horses over a single road. Or how much money the shipowners were losing, and the sailors and dock-workers, out of work as they were. They just thought it was a great joke to watch a grand English officer as he shook back his lace ruffles, opening his jeweled snuff box to take a pinch, and then see his face turn red as he stopped to stare at a herd of cattle lumbering through the city street.

Once the children, hanging around wherever anything was going on, saw a big flock of sheep, driven in by an old farmer in his shirt sleeves, leather apron, homespun breeches, and home-knit wool stockings. Around them they heard the grownups say, "Why, that's General Putnam. Old Put himself. Come all the way from Connecticut."

The Boston people on the street called out to him through the dust raised by his flock's pattering little feet. The old fellow nodded, smiled, and lifted his long crook-necked staff to show he had heard.

"Who's he, Paul?" the younger Revere children asked their big brother.

Young Paul knew from having heard the talk of his father and his friends. "He's the militia officer who was in command of our soldiers when Fort Ticonderoga was taken. He fought there beside Lord Howe."

"Oh," cried the children astonished, "is he British? He doesn't look it."

"No, no, in those days our American militia was fighting alongside the Regulars, you know, the way Father did at Fort William Henry."

"But how could——" the children began.

Young Paul put his finger to his lips to make them stop talking. A train of wagons going along a side street had halted the old farmer and his sheep. As they waited, a little group of British officers came along. When they saw who the shepherd was, one of them called out to him in a joking way, "Well, General Putnam, you old fire-eater! Do we get the pleasure of a visit from you because you smell gunpowder in the air, ancient warrior?"

Another said laughingly, "Just wait a few days and there'll be enough in the air for anybody. We expect twenty warships with supplies and twenty regiments to come in from England any day now."

Over his dusty sheep the old farmer looked seriously into the gay faces of the men in scarlet uniforms. "If they come," he said with dignity, "*if* they come, I am prepared to treat them as enemies."

He waved his crook, his sheep went pattering ahead, he walking sturdily behind them.

"Oh! *la*——!" whispered a Boston lady behind the Revere children, looking at the faces, blank and stony now, of the British officers.

Yes, there was something interesting for children to watch every one of the days their parents found so dark. On the Common, there were always British troops, fine in their well-cut scarlet uniforms and

flashing buttons, snapping to attention when their
officers barked out orders, now marching straight forward, now on a slant to the left or to the right, now
slowly, now suddenly running forward, their fero-
ciously sharp bayonets pointed ahead. Or perhaps, at
one single shouted command, spinning around on their
heels and marching straight back in the opposite direction. It was as good as any show you'd have to pay
to see, the Revere children thought.

But one thing they never were allowed to stay to
see—the flogging of those soldiers who had tried to
desert and had been caught. Their big brother had
strict orders to bring the children home and come into
the house and shut the door tight, the minute he saw
the Negro drummers, long whips in their hands,
marching out behind some soldiers with their hands tied.

Their father said, "I'm ashamed even to have you
know such things are done. I will not have you see
them done."

But of course the children heard from others what
happened—men whipped until they fainted, till they
. . .

"Stop that talk!" their father called out. "You live
in America. We don't beat men to death here."

For it was not just men being whipped that so
shocked the Americans. A man in their own militia who
had done something wrong was whipped, that being a
common punishment in those days. But never more
than thirty-nine strokes. And the British floggings were
two hundred, three hundred, five hundred, eight—well,

Paul Revere was right. It's nothing to be talked about.

The British were trying by such terrible punishments to keep their soldiers from deserting. But they went right on doing it. There were fewer out to drill every day. General Gage sent for more troops from England. They came. But soon life in America looked pretty good to some of them. The British officers were shocked that so many of them slipped away to live as Americans. Some of these well-trained soldiers even helped to drill the American Militia, teaching them many important points.

For the militia was drilling as never before. Everywhere in Massachusetts towns and villages, the men and big boys were out, learning how to handle themselves as soldiers, how to march. They were already pretty good shots because there was so much game left in the new country. Many of them were hunters.

About this time a certain number of every troop of militia agreed to be ready for service at a minute's notice. They were called Minute Men. To live up to this name, they never went to bed in their low-ceilinged, plain little bedrooms without laying out their clothes and their guns, powder-horns, and bullets within reach. In a minute they could be dressed, downstairs and out of the house, ready to fight.

Paul Revere, watching these simple country people harden themselves as best they could against whatever they were going to have to do, thought of Aunt Barb's story from the Bible.

None of this could be hidden. Nobody in Massachusetts wanted to hide it. The British General Gage knew about it. And since he was an old campaigner, he also knew that there was no better way of keeping people from fighting than by taking away their guns and ammunition. He began planning to get hold of the small amounts of powder and bullets and guns which the militia had got together outside of Boston. Very early one morning in September 1774, he sent his soldiers out to Cambridge and took, by surprise, a couple of cannon and two hundred and fifty kegs of gunpowder.

This made a great stir among the American Militia, among everybody in New England. Those kegs of gunpowder belonged to the militia—so the militia thought. American money had paid for them. What right had English troops to take them? Old General Putnam scolded them like schoolboys for not having been on guard. "Don't you let that happen again!" he said.

The word got round that General Gage had said the American Militia had tried to keep the Regulars from taking the powder, but had run like rabbits at the sight of the British bayonets. As a matter of fact, the Americans didn't get to the spot till after the Regulars were safely back in Boston.

There were also kegs of powder and muskets stored at the fort in Portsmouth, New Hampshire, about sixty miles from Boston. In December the British made plans to send some of their troops up there to bring these back. But by this time Paul Revere had "got up another gang." The special business of this group was to find out what the British were up to. They were out every night in the Boston streets, walking around, up and down, sauntering, their hands in their pockets, looking like anybody else, but keeping their eyes and ears open. In this way they found out that General Gage was planning to send troops to Portsmouth to bring back those war materials.

On December twelfth Paul Revere went off on horseback to warn the Portsmouth Minute Men. He rode sixty miles, all night and most of the next day, over bad roads that were no more than frozen mud and ruts. But he got there in time. In a minute the militiamen turned out, as they had said they would, went to the fort and brought away 97 barrels of powder and 100 muskets.

When the news of this reached London, the King was in a rage. If he had been furious with Massachusetts before, he was forty times as angry now. General Gage was scolded, and ordered never to let this happen again. He was to go out into the country around Boston and bring in every bit of the war supplies the American Militia had collected, wherever it was.

So General Gage sent a colonel up to Salem with 150 soldiers to get some arms that were hidden there. The British didn't know any better than to do this in broad daylight, on a Sunday. Of course, in no time, the word got around. The call for militia was given by the church bells ringing wildly, by drums booming in every village, by express riders galloping at top speed along the side roads. The armed Minute Men swarmed along the roads to Salem and got there about as soon as the British did.

The British colonel thought better of his idea. There were too many armed fighters there, and more coming in every minute. Too many of all kinds of Americans, for everybody in Salem, man, woman, child and baby turned out to call the British names and make fun of them.

It had been a mistake, the colonel thought, to try to make such an expedition by day. The next time an effort was made to take war supplies from the colonial militia, it had better be by night. So he would recommend to General Gage when he got back to Boston.

The next time was Concord.

A Last Family Talk in the Shop

17

IN THE dusky shop, only one tallow candle alight, Paul Revere was talking very quietly to his wife and oldest son. Quietly because he very much did not wish anyone else to hear what he was saying. Also because he always spoke quietly and kindly to his family, as his father had spoken to him.

But what he was saying was not at all quiet. For this was the evening of Tuesday, April 18th, 1775.

"It's to Concord they're going now. To get the powder and arms and flour our militia has stored there." (He did not need to say that he meant the British when he said "they.") "They start tonight."

"Are you sure? How do you know?" His wife's lips formed the words almost without a sound.

"Plenty of ways to find out. There's a British private whose wife works for Mrs. Stedman. They both live in the Stedman house. His sergeant called there this afternoon to tell him to report at eight o'clock. Bottom of the Common. Ready for active service. A stableboy told me that horses were ordered this afternoon for a picked lot of officers. They have already crossed over to Cambridge. He heard them talking while he was putting on the saddles. They said they are going to string out along the road towards Lexington and Concord to keep any rider from getting through to give the alarm."

"But Father, *you*'re going?"

"Yes, son. I'm going. Another express rider and I are going to try it."

His wife said, "But Paul, Dawes is in no such danger as you. He's not known to the British."

"What'll you do, Father, with all those officers watching the road?"

"The best I can, son."

"Now Paul," his wife reminded him, "you *were* at Concord, day before yesterday. You told them that probably the Regulars' next trip would be to get the militia stores there. They *are* warned."

" 'Probably' isn't good enough, Rachel. That powder and cannon and all the rest will be taken by surprise unless the Minute Men are called tonight—long enough in advance to get there with their muskets."

Paul's wife tried to hope, "Maybe the Regulars won't really shoot this time," she murmured. "Last September they took the militia cannon and all that gunpowder at Cambridge, and got back to Boston and never fired a shot. Nobody got hurt."

Paul frowned and winced at the memory, "I'm ashamed of that. The Minute Men hadn't had warning. They didn't get there fast enough. We mustn't ever let that happen again. When he heard about that, Old General Putnam sent word to us to take better care of our gun-powder. I'll never forget what the old fellow wrote: 'Powder must be the great means, under God, of the salvation of our country'."

"But at Salem—the Regulars just marched out and stood around and marched back again. They didn't even try to get the militia stores," persisted Paul's wife, in an even lower murmur.

"They made that Salem try in broad daylight. On a Sunday, too, with the streets full of people. Everybody all along the way saw them from the minute they started. Everybody gave the alarm. The church bells rang like mad. Express riders were out as fast as the saddles could be thrown on the horses. The Minute Men came swarming. The Regulars saw they were outnumbered. There was nothing for them to do but to turn around and get back to Boston."

"Maybe that'll happen this time."

"Yes, dear girl, maybe it will. If Dawes and I can get out the Minute Men in time. But now the Regulars go by night. Everybody along the way will be sound asleep when they come."

"Unless you wake them up, Father."

Paul nodded. "Yes, that's the point. If we can get the church bells clanging, and plenty of muskets shot off to give the alarm, and if enough of the Minute Men line up to look dangerous, maybe the Regulars will turn back this time, too, without shooting."

Something in his voice made his wife say anxiously, "But maybe not."

"Yes, dear wife, maybe not," he spoke seriously.

His wife's thin, white face grew paler. His teen-age son's eyes never left Paul's. There was a short heavy silence.

The three of them, like all Boston people who were not on the side of the British, were half-starved. In spite of food brought in by land, there had not been enough to eat in Boston all during those months of being shut up in the city with no ships bringing food, and with no wages earned. Boston people were indeed being punished by the King for the Tea-Party.

"When will you be back, Paul?"

"Can't tell, Rachel. This time I may be caught, you know."

"Oh *Father*—if you're caught—what'll——"

"I may be shot, son, or hanged. This is real rebellion now. And rebels get hanged."

Paul spoke these dark words as quietly as any others. But his son's young face crumpled up in horror.

Paul Revere laid his hand on the big boy's shoulder. "Look, son, if I were a rich man I'd be making my will now, to be sure you'd inherit what I've got to leave you. I'm not a rich man, so I'll just tell you now what I've got to leave you. It'll be all you'll have from me, and it's enough for anybody. My father handed it on to me from his father, and I pass it along to you: Listen, nobody with a brave heart needs to know beforehand that he's surely going to win. If he's any good, all he needs is just one fighting chance to win.

"And as for being hanged, we all have to die, son, sometime. You can't dodge that. The important thing is to be ready to die bravely, whether you stop a bullet when you're young, or die in your bed of old age—or get hanged in a good cause."

A low knock came on the door. Paul went to open it with his usual, firm, light step. A plainly dressed young man in a blackened leather apron stood outside, his fair tousled head bare. "Mr. Revere," he said in a whispering secret voice, "I've been down at the Common. A lot of them are gathering. They are all armed for active service." He looked over his shoulder, and went on, "It is said they are starting for Concord."

"Thanks to you, Ned," said Paul Revere. "You're the third to bring that news in the past hour. I'm glad to be sure of it. William Dawes is starting by land, to see if he can get out. And I'll be on my way in a few minutes."

Now the young blacksmith spoke out, in clear, ringing voice. "God keep you, Mr. Revere!" he said
earnestly.

"Amen," said Mrs. Revere from inside the house.

The door closed. Paul Revere reached for his long-
skirted riding-coat. His wife came quickly with his hat.
He already had his riding boots on. His son handed
him the woolen muffler. "No need for that," he said.
"It's a mild April night."

"I thought you might wind it around your face, so
they wouldn't know you."

"I'm proud to show my face on this work and I want
you to be proud of what I'm doing. And listen, *you
make the younger children understand.*"

"Oh, Father, they're not interested. They only want
to run around and play."

"They have more sense than you think. They must
understand. What we are doing won't make any sense
unless the children remember it. It's not worth doing
if they don't understand. I leave you that as your part
of the work. Do it."

He took his wife's hand and his son's. "If the two of
you stand firm, you can keep life together for the
family. It may be a long time before we see each other
again. Son, you're pretty young to be the man of the
family. But you're three years older than your French
grandfather was when he stood up and went on alone
to whatever he had to face. And never forget, it's something to be proud of, all your life—and happy about—
that we have the *chance* to fight for what we think is

right. There's something for me to do in this fight. So
I'm a happy and a proud man this night—even if I am
scared."

He looked it, his black eyes fiery bright, his dark
face glowing, a smile on his lips.

He was off, letting himself carefully out of the door
into the moonlit street.

The woman and the big boy looked after him. They
could barely make him out. But for a long time they
could hear the sound of his steady booted steps on the
cobblestones.

They shut the door. "Mother, how is he even going to
get started on his ride? There are all those sentries. The
other rider is going by land, the roundabout way. But
Father's going by Charlestown. How'll he get across?"

"They have a small boat hidden under the rocks on
the North Shore."

"Where'll he get a horse? Ours is out in the barn."

"The Committee of Safety at Charlestown have one
ready."

"But the British have brought up their big ship. It's
anchored right where Father's boat will have to go.
They're going to shoot at anybody who tries to get
across."

"Your father will take care not to have any noise
made. Maybe the watch on the frigate won't see them.
A small boat close to the water isn't plain at night.
They don't keep a very good watch, you know. They
don't think they need to. They often play the fool, and

forget everything except betting on their card games or drinking. The British have been told ever so many times that they can do what they please to Americans because we're all cowards."

She had found the right word. The boy's anxious white face flushed. He flung his head up; his eyes flashed like his father's. He doubled his fists. "We'll show them," he said in a loud, rough voice.

"I hope we will, son," said Mrs. Revere, soberly, "but right now the thing to do is to go to bed, so we can be up early for a good day's work. We Reveres have our livings to earn, you know."

The Two Lanterns

18

IN THE dark, in front of the house of Robert Newman, sexton of Christ Church, Paul Revere slowed down. He could see through the lighted windows that the front room of the Newman house was filled with British officers. They were doing what Boston people mostly saw them doing—playing cards, drinking and having a loud, jolly time together. How could a man known to the English get at the sexton without being seen? As he hesitated, a man standing in a shadowy corner of the street began to walk casually along. When he reached Paul Revere, he said in a low tone, "Go ahead. I'll follow you." It was the sexton. Paul stepped forward.

The two men were alone in the street. Over his shoulder Paul asked, "How did you get out? Did they see you?"

The sexton answered, "Out of a window. Over a shed-roof. No, they didn't."

Nothing more was said until they turned, in front of the old church. Another man was waiting in the shadow there. He was to stand guard, while the sexton climbed up the long steps of the tower.

The three men stood close to the door of the church and talked in whispers. "How long shall I leave the lanterns in the window, Mr. Revere?"

"That's hard to say. Not long. I've told the Charlestown people to be on the lookout. So remember, not a glimmer till the lanterns are in the window. British sentries on the ship are watching and our chances are better if the British don't guess what we're up to."

The man who was to stand guard broke in anxiously, "But Mr. Revere, a light won't hurt as long as it's inside. Climbing in the dark he'll risk breaking his neck."

"No he won't," said Paul. "I know every inch of the tower. The steps are all right so long as you keep well over to the left side with a hand against the wall to guide you. There's an opening where the bells hang.

The patrol on the Somerset might catch a flash through the cracks . . . or our watchers at Charlestown might think it showed a single lantern, and start off before you got the two hung out. We can't take any chances." He turned to the sexton. "Now, remember, two lanterns. I told the Charlestown Committee it would be two if the Regulars start by boat."

"I hope they see it, Mr. Revere, it's a long way to Charlestown."

"They'll see it," answered Paul. "I was a bell ringer here when I was a boy. Many's the time I've looked over at Charlestown from the top of this tower. And back at it from Charlestown. I know just the place over there where you can get a clear view. The Committee will be there, watching. They'll catch the first gleam."

The other asked, "But you are on your way to Charlestown now. Why are signals needed?"

"I'm on my way. But I may never get there. If my boat is sighted from the Somerset, it'll be sunk by shot. If I don't get over to them, the Charlestown Committee is to send another rider out to try to get through with the alarm."

The sexton murmured respectfully, "It's a great risk you are taking."

"I'm not the only one. You're doing as much. If they ever find out who hung those signals, you'll land in Boston Jail."

"I'm proud to take that risk, Mr. Revere."

"So am I," said Revere heartily. He went on. "Now

remember, it must be two lanterns you show. Be sure
to hang them well apart so the Charlestown folks can
be sure there are two of them."

The sexton unlocked the church door, paused a moment, and said in a loud voice, "God help you this
night, Mr. Revere."

"Amen!" said the other man.

The sexton pulled the door shut and locked it. The
man on guard took his position in the shadow of the
church door, looking up and down the empty street.

Paul Revere walked steadily on to whatever was before him—shooting, hanging, or glory.

Near the place where his boat was hidden, two men
sauntering in the mild April evening on different sides
of the street, turned when they saw him. The three
men walked separately as though they had no connec-
tion with each other. It was a quiet part of the city.
Nobody noticed them as, one by one, they turned into a
dark alley.

They did not come out. Now they were in a small
boat, the two men at the oars. In the stern sat Paul
Revere, very straight, very still. Just below the
handles, the oars were wrapped in flannel, at the place
where they rub against the oarlocks as they are pulled
to and fro, so the usual clinking noise was muffled.
They made not a sound. But of course, as they were
dipped in and out of the water, the wet blades flashed
in the light from the rising moon. No help for that.

Not a word was said. They knew what to do—to

keep as far away as they could from the ship with its sixty-four guns. Paul Revere kept his head turned towards the great warship and those guns.

How could the watch on the frigate help seeing the boat? The moon was not yet risen but he himself could see, easily enough, the lines of boats beyond the ship, going back and forth ferrying the Regulars across to Cambridge. No others were to be allowed out that night. If anybody on the deck of the tall ship should happen to glance around, he couldn't help seeing the telltale silver flash of those wet oars. How could that flash be missed by a watch set there to make sure no boat was out?

The silent men at the oars knew they were risking their lives. They pulled steadily towards the Charlestown shore. The silent man, sitting straight and easy at the stern, did not take his eyes from the anchored ship looming up tall, black, threatening. From its guns, at any instant, death might dart out at him.

Where could the British patrols be? Perhaps all gathered on the other side to watch the boats carrying the troops to Cambridge? Or one of them might have caught sight, already, of the forbidden attempt to cross. Perhaps one of the guns was being leveled at them this instant. He sat motionless, breathing deeply, wondering if they had now gone far enough so that he could swim to the Charlestown side—if he were not killed in the first fire from the ship. His fixed gaze on the huge black hulk of the Somerset shifted with a jerk. Something else had come into view. He caught sight of an object near them. He turned his head cautiously. It was a tree! Why, there was land, close at hand. They were getting near to the Charlestown side. They hadn't been seen. Was it possible that they hadn't been seen?

Still without a word, the men at the oars pulled in closer and closer to the stony beach. Paul Revere gathered the long skirts of his riding coat around him. The bottom of the boat grazed the stones. The oarsmen lifted the oars and looked at him. The moment had come. They had made it.

Their pause was but an instant. In one powerful leap, their passenger was out of the boat. They rowed on without him. They rounded the point. They were out of sight. They were still alive, as they had hardly hoped they would be when they had pushed off from the Boston shore.

Paul Revere was still alive too, his skin crawling with taut suspense. He drew a long breath, took off his hat, passed his hand over the back of his neck to smooth down those hairs that had seemed to stand up coldly as he braced himself against death. He put his hat back on, and walked steadily up the sloping shore. He knew where to go. And shortly he had found his way through the dark to the Charlestown house where he was expected.

They told him that his signals had been seen. They had a horse waiting for him. But all roads, they said, were watched by British officers on horseback.

"There are back roads," he said. "Short cuts through the fields. I know them, the British don't."

They brought out the horse, saddled and bridled. He took one look at the fine animal—he never forgot what a good horse it was—and thought to himself that no heavy British army mount could compare with it.

"If I see them before they see me. . . ." he thought.

One of the Charlestown men said he had already tried to send a messenger out to Lexington to give the warning. But he shook his head sadly. "I doubt that my man will ever get through the British net. He's probably been picked up by some of those officers by this time. Has William Dawes started?"

"He was to try to get out through the English sentries on the Neck. I don't know if he made it."

They've strung a net around Boston like a spider's web. Dawes will never slip through."

Paul Revere thought, standing by that fine fleet horse, the reins in his hand, "I'll get through. *If I see them first. . . ."*

He was in the saddle. The little knot of men looked up at him. The moon had fully risen now. They saw him plainly. Would they ever see him again? Everything now depended on Revere. Would he get through? Could he get through? Would he perhaps at the very first turn of the road be captured or forced to turn back?

They held up their hands in a gesture of goodbye. Now there was nothing more to say. The man on the horse nodded silently and rode away at a sober, careful, rapid trot. In the saddle from which he might be shot down at any moment, he sat as straight as he had in the boat during the perilous trip across the water. They stood looking after him till there was nothing to see but darkness. Would he get through? Would they ever see him again?

On Moonlit Roads

19

THE man on the horse fixed his mind on one thought: *"I must see them first."*

He must not ride so fast that he would run into an ambush. He must not ride so slowly that those red-coated troops now being landed could reach the first village before he did. For it would be enough, although not all he wanted, if he could reach even the first few farmhouses on the road to Lexington before the Reg-

ulars did. Just let him rouse two or three families, and
tell them the British were on the way. The alarm
would be passed along, to those beyond. The Minute
Men would spring to their arms. The boys too young
to carry a gun would be off on horseback to wake up
people who lived on lanes and back roads and to get
other big boys to go farther. The old men would start
the drums beating so they could be heard for miles,
would pull furiously on the ropes of the church bells
to throw out their wild summons to fight. Yes, it would
be enough if he could get through the empty wasteland
back of Charlestown to the first cluster of houses, at a
crossroads. Let him be shot down there—he would
have done what he was out to do.

But what he wanted was to get through to Lexington. Two of the most important men on the American
side—Samuel Adams and John Hancock—were in Lexington. The British hoped to take them by surprise. If
they did, they'd be sent back to London to be hanged
for treason—as Paul would be if he were caught. He
felt that come what might, he *must* get through to the
first settlement. If he possibly could, he must reach Lexington to make sure the two leaders of the Americans
were safe. And it would be well if he could go on from
there to Concord, although the alarm, if he could start
it, might well have spread to that town without him.

That was what he intended to do. He knew he could
do it—*if he could only see the British patrols before
they saw him.*

As he rode out over the empty moorland back of

Charlestown, there was not a sound except the hoof-beats of his horse, trotting cautiously when he came to a place where trees or bushes cast a shadow, let out to a full run on open stretches clear in the moonlight. The patrols would never show themselves in the open. They would hide in the shadows.

His keen black eyes ranged everywhere at once, searching the distance, focused intently on every dusky thicket beside the road. At any instant, just as in the boat, a shot might leap out at him. And now not only from one place on which he could keep his eyes. From anywhere. From either side of the road, behind him, from in front of him. But how much better this was, with something active he could do, than that dreadful passage on the water, sitting helpless, the hair on the back of his neck rising in suspense.

He checked his speed to peer sharply around a turn of the road, he loosened the reins, touched his mount's flanks with the spurs, and leaned forward over the mane as the horse broke into a run.

Nobody knows what thoughts went through his mind in that desperate race. Did he remember again that if he were caught he would be hanged? Did he remember his father's saying that all a brave man needs is a fighting chance, just one?

We don't know. But we do know, as though we were inside his mind, that one thought a man might have had never once occurred to him—the simple idea that all he had to do to be safe was just to turn his horse into the thick woods, anywhere. He could stay there, hidden, till everything was all over—whatever that night might bring. He was alone. Nobody was there to see what he did. Nobody would ever know. He could say the British patrols chased him into the woods and he lost his way.

He rode straight ahead, his quick eyes shifting from side to side of the road, his quick mind flashing over what he knew of British ways.

Any man of sense who had fought Indians, if he were set to guard a road on a moonlit night, would cover up anything on his clothes that might catch the light. But Revere thought of Braddock, of the British soldiers he had seen at Albany, of those he had watched drilling on the Common at Boston. He was sure that no British officer would ever spoil the looks of his uniform by covering up a well-polished buckle, a white strap or a cockade. So, as he rode on, trotting cautiously, or galloping wildly, he watched for anything that might show white or catch the light. *He must see them first.*

He did.

Under those trees, what was that white patch? Nothing natural was as white as that. And that gleam, as from something brightly polished? His quick hands drew his horse to a stop.

He saw them now. Two officers on horseback, almost invisible in the shadow cast by a tree. The white came from their ribbon cockades. The reflected gleam was from the pistol holsters kept so brilliantly shiny by the common soldiers who did the work for them.

Now the officers had seen him too, in spite of his dark

coat, dark hair and pulled-down black hat. They had a
plan to stop him. One of them launched his horse plunging straight at him. The other turned and dashed off up
the road to head him off if the first one did not make
the capture.

But Paul Revere had seen them first!

He swung his horse about, and struck in the spurs. In
the instant of time since his eye had caught that first
gleam of white, his ready mind had made a plan to fit
that exact place. He would go straight cross-country at
top speed, to another road.

As clearly as though it were before him on a map, he
saw exactly what fields to cross, what stone walls to
leap—and there was a pond, with clay banks that were
slippery. He would know how to dodge that, with his
little native-born horse. The Britisher on his great military charger would not.

He was off. The officer was taken aback at the idea
of leaving the road, but spurred his handsome mount to
follow. Again Paul Revere's back hairs crawled on his
neck, as his taut body expected a shot from behind. But
his mind knew no fear.

He kept his horse galloping at full speed, he watched
the rough field over which they were racing, but he
turned his head just enough so that he could see from
the side of his eye where the British officer was. He
was no nearer than in that instant on the road when
he had sprung out to block the way. He was farther.
Yes, he was dropping behind!

Paul leaned low over his horse's neck, put his weight

well forward, kept his eyes fixed on the ground ahead rushing up towards them, dropping behind. Huckleberry bushes, great rocks, a clump of trees. There was the pond—its banks treacherously covered with grass. He swung his horse far to one side and felt, to his joy, a clatter of stony ground under those flying hooves. Behind him the British horse had gone straight ahead over what looked like grass land, had slipped when its feet struck the clay, was sliding down the bank, plunging and floundering wildly. His rider, thrown to one side of the saddle, struggled to get his balance.

Paul Revere shook out the bridle and gave his horse his head. He had almost come through to the Mystic River. Once there, he would find a wooden bridge into the first village on the road to Lexington. If he could only get as far as that.

Through the trees, he saw a road! It was a little country road. Did the British know about it? Would it be patrolled? Before leaving the woods, he drew rein to look up and down. The road was empty. He took his horse out on it in a run, raced down to the bridge and galloped across, the loose planks rattling under those flying feet.

He was in Medford. He had made it. He was alive.

The village lay dark and sleeping in the night just as it would have been—defenseless—a few hours later, if he had not come through.

None of us need ever hope to be happier than Paul Revere was as he galloped his horse down that dark

village street and along the lane till he came to the
home of the captain of the Medford Minute Men. He
leaned from his saddle to hammer on the door with the
handle of his whip. A window flew up. Through the
dark came Paul Revere's shout, *"The Regulars are out!*
On their way to Concord."

That was enough. Everyone knew what was meant
by that cry. Knew what to do. Was ready to do it. Before Paul was even back on the road, one half-dressed
boy was racing for the church to ring the tocsin bell, an
old man with silvery hair had stepped from the next
house, his drumsticks flying on his drum, another boy
was in a barn saddling a horse. Lights came on in houses.
Windows were flying up.

"The Regulars are out," shouted the dark rider to
one side or the other, as he raced by. "Start a boy up
to Cobble Hill to give the alarm there."

"The Regulars are out. On their way to Concord.
Get somebody over the Menot Flats, to those houses."

"The Regulars are out."

A wave of hatred flowed over those country hearts
at that name.

"The Regulars are out." The village was flaming in
excitement, the Minute Men were running from their
houses, muskets in their hands, to form a line on the
Common, ready to head for Lexington and Concord.

On the moonlit road beyond the village, the man on
horseback rode hard. Sometimes before he reached a
house, the swift beat of his horse's hooves, loud in the
silent night, had wakened the people in a sleeping

home. If a light showed in a window, if a head was thrust out, he did not draw rein, but shouted as he passed, *"The Regulars are out. Give the alarm."* If there was no sign of life, he rode up to the door and hammered on it fiercely till someone from inside called back. Then, "The Regulars are out. Get the alarm going," and he rode on, sure of what would follow.

House after house sprang from sleep to action. Mile after mile the rider covered at headlong speed. Then as he came to the top of a slope, there was the town of Lexington.

It was after midnight. The two American leaders were asleep in the minister's house where they were lodged. A sergeant's squad had been set to watch the house. When Revere came thundering in, they sprang up to stop him. Not a soul there yet knew what Paul Revere had come through to tell them.

"The Regulars are out," shouted Revere.

He was heard inside the house. His voice was known. John Hancock called out, "Come in, Revere." The door opened, he went in, and exploded his great bomb of news. Behind him one of the guard had run across to the church. As he told his story, the bell began to clang out its alarm. He raised his voice to be heard over its loud pealing.

"Over a thousand British troops are on the way. I saw them when I left Boston at ten o'clock tonight. Crossing the river in boats. They may arrive any moment now. The alarm has been given, all round about. The Minute Men are arming and gathering."

There was a wild hurry in the house as the two men, so vital to the American side, made ready to leave.

Half an hour later, William Dawes rode in. He had bribed his way past a sentry on the "Neck," shaken off one patrol and ridden the roundabout road through Roxbury. The two express riders were well satisfied with their night's work. They had a bite to eat, took a drink, and considered what to do next.

As his wife had reminded him, Paul had taken orders from the Committee of Safety to Concord only two days before. Most of their military stores were already hidden. And as for the alarm, that had already spread far and wide. Near and far they could hear bells tolling and muskets fired as warning signals. Just the same, they wanted to finish what they had started.

Paul and Dawes turned their horses towards Concord, and a young Dr. Prescott rode along with them. He lived in the district, knew everyone and all the lanes and byroads.

This time, halfway to Concord, there were not two, but four British officers suddenly blocking the way. The Americans were forced into a field where six more British were waiting. In the darkness and confusion Dawes slid off his horse and managed to hide in the bushes. Prescott jumped a stone wall and rode off. But Paul was squarely cornered with a pistol cold against his forehead.

"Who are you? Where do you come from?"

Paul thought quickly. Someone might recognize him.

Boldness was his only hope. "My name's Revere," he said. "I left Boston about ten o'clock."

They could hardly believe him. It was only just past midnight. How could anyone have made such quick time? But at his name they broke out into angry words and threats.

Then a bell, quite near, started ringing. The British looked at one another, worried. They quieted down and one of them, remembering orders, tried to explain why they were here. "We're only out after deserters," he said.

Paul saw his chance. "I know better. I know what you're after. But you won't get it. The alarm has been given everywhere. And it's spreading."

The British put their heads together and talked in tones too low for Paul Revere to hear. Then they took the reins out of his hands and led his horse in their midst back along the road to Lexington. The major waved his pistol and said, "As for you, Paul Revere, don't try to escape or I'll blow your brains out. You go back with us. We'll send you to England to be tried and hanged for treason."

Paul answered briefly. "Do as you like about that. But what chance have you to get to Boston? There are only ten of you. Your troops are hours away. There are at least five hundred Minute Men heading here at this minute. In an hour there will be thousands more."

It was slow work leading Revere's horse. The road was dark and lonely. The Englishmen got uneasy and alarmed. With good reason. What chance did they have against a whole countryside swarming with armed men who hated them?

All at once a gun was fired. In the darkness, it rang out very loud. The officers drew their horses sharply to a halt.

"What was that?" the British major snapped out.

"Only another alarm gun. They're being fired like that everywhere from here to Connecticut. You've a mighty slim chance of getting back to Boston with whole skins." Revere spoke out boldly though he knew he was still in mortal danger.

The British officers had another short whispered talk. "Dismount," they told him. As Revere had hoped, they began to see that they had a better chance to escape without being burdened with a prisoner.

They mounted one of their sergeants on Paul's horse and, spurring their mounts to a run, vanished down the road.

The Shot Heard 'Round the World

20

PERHAPS here is as good a place as any other to remember that Paul Revere was not a person in a storybook. He was a real man. One of the differences between a book-invention and a live human being is this: The author who has made up a character can end his story the minute it stops being exciting. A real person goes on living.

Certainly Paul Revere went on living. He was forty

years old that night in April, 1775 when the British
officers rode hurriedly on and left him standing in his
riding-boots alone, in the dark, on that country road.
He had forty-three more years before him. He had
been in deadly danger nearly every minute of the time
since, at ten-o'clock the evening before, he stepped into
the hidden boat. He had made a wild ride, risking his
life for the new cause of freedom and independence.
Everything had depended on getting a warning to the
Minute Men to turn out. He had done his part. His
great adventure was over.

He must have been as tired as any man could be. He
was not young. He had ridden like mad. He had been
terribly excited. You'd think he'd have felt like dropping down anywhere to rest.

He could have rested. It was a mild spring night. He
could have stepped into the woods to lie down under a
tree. Nobody would have known about it. If it had
been known, nobody would have blamed him. Or he
could have walked on till he came to a barn, and have
gone to sleep on the dry, soft hay.

You might think he'd have felt, "Now I've done *my*
share! That's enough."

What he really did was to think, *"Now* what more
can I do? I'll go and see."

He had no horse. But he knew the shortcuts. He sat
down on a rock, took off his spurs, put them in his
pocket and struck off through the open country. In his
heavy riding boots, he trudged through the dark, over
the fields, till he was once more back in Lexington.

Dawn was just showing grey. In the church steeple the bell was still ringing to summon the Minute Men. The British Regulars had not yet come, but they were close at hand.

"What can I do now?" The weary express rider stood ready for anything.

There *was* something to do. A plain, small piece of work it was; but both dangerous and very much needed. Mr. Hancock, the American leader, had left upstairs in a nearby house, a trunk full of papers, documents, letters, records, lists of names, and files, all about the American resistance to the British King. These must not fall into the hands of the Regulars.

As readily as he had swung up into the saddle at Charlestown, Revere took on this expressman's job. The trunk was too heavy for one man to carry. Mr. Hancock's secretary went with him. To get to the house, they passed across the grassy open place called the Green in front of the church. In the simple wooden homes set around the Green, everybody was awake, although it was only about four in the morning. Women and children, their faces very pale, looked out of the windows at their menfolks drawn up in a line on the grass. Some Minute Men were already there; more were coming in. They were not in uniform but hastily dressed in their everyday work clothes. The American Militia had not enough muskets to go around. Some of these farmers and blacksmiths and merchants had muskets. Other had no arms at all. Paul Revere passed through the lines of waiting men. Waiting? What for? They did not know. Nobody knew what would take place in the next few minutes. But everybody felt that what did happen would change history. And it did.

Paul Revere walked so close to these plain country people he could have touched their homespun clothes, their battered old guns, no two alike. He looked into their set faces as they gazed across the Green, at the road up which at that very moment the British were steadily marching. By the time he and his helper had dashed in at the back door of the house where Hancock's trunk had been left, the British Regulars were marching past it. So it happened that Paul Revere looked almost directly from those sixty or seventy fellow-Americans of his, simply dressed, badly armed, to the full might, majesty and power of the army of a great nation. From the second-story window he looked down upon hundreds of them, rank after rank of scarlet uniforms, brilliantly polished brass buttons, fine muskets, each one with its fiercely shining, sharp, steel bayonet-blade. They stepped along powerfully, all their legs moving together. The officers, their bright uniforms brighter with gold lace, rode proudly on horses rubbed to a silky sheen by their servants. Did Aunt Barb's comforting reminder of David and Goliath come to Paul's mind? Or did his heart sink?

Probably neither.

Carrying his end of the trunk, he and his helper were down again on the Green. They passed once again close to the lines of waiting militiamen. Their captain was saying—Paul Revere heard this with his own ears, and never forgot it—"Let the troops pass. Don't molest them without they begin first."

Hurrying with the trunk, he was around the corner, off the Green. Here is what he wrote later. "A gun was fired. I heard the report and turned my head. But I could see only the Regulars. I saw smoke in front of them. They gave a great shout, ran forward a few paces, and then they all fired."

Paul Revere saw no more of the battle of Lexington. He had that trunk to carry to safety, so he carried it.

You probably know what happened the rest of that day. It is all told in the first American history book an American reads in school. The War for Independence began, then and there, that very minute. The volley of musket-shots seen over his shoulder by Paul Revere, as he lugged that trunk along, was the first firing on American militia done by the British Army. Eight of the Minute Men were killed. Ten were wounded. One British soldier had his leg slightly grazed by a bullet.

After they had sent those bullets blazing into the men in lines before them, the British soldiers shouted and cheered joyfully at the top of their voices. "Hurrah! hurrah!" All winter long they had been cooped up in Boston doing nothing. It seemed fine to be out, each with a loaded gun to fire, doing what they felt regular armies are for—killing people.

After these loud shouts of pleasure, they left the dead and wounded Americans, some of them lying in their own dooryards, and marched on to Concord. They made a fine show all the way, their cockades fresh and snow-white, their uniforms fitting neatly, their legs swinging forward in the powerful *"left,* right, *left,* right"* of men who know how to march as soldiers should march.

They swung smartly along that old country road towards Concord, with the rising sun bringing out the color and sparkle of the military picture they made— only there was nobody to see them but the woodchucks in the fields and the robins in the trees. And all this time the Minute Men were coming in on the run to Concord. The alarm that had been started by Revere was spreading faster and faster, farther and farther, as the circles spread, widening, when you throw a stone into a pool.

By the time they reached Concord, the militia had swarmed in by hundreds. Not just sixty or seventy half-armed men standing motionless like those the British had fired on in Lexington; these were soldiers with rifles and powder, who knew how to fight.

They did fight. At the North Bridge just outside of Concord. This time the British fell back, outnumbered, and joined the other troops in Concord. There were so many Minute Men out now that the English officers decided to get their troops back to Boston, as they had from Salem two months before.

But by this time, people had heard about the deaths at Lexington, and the joyful hurrahing of the Regulars over having, at last, a chance to fire at and kill Americans. The militia were wild with rage and sorrow over the deaths of their fellow-patriots, and began firing on the British as they started to retreat. Your history books tell you how the marching British found themselves outnumbered and fired on from every direction at once, from behind stone walls, from trees, from any cover there was. Before they had gone far, they were stepping faster and faster. And then they began to run for dear life. They had a long way to go before they could reach the protection of the British forces in Boston.

If Paul Revere was still in Lexington when they passed through on their way back, he had a third picture to remember, very different from the other two he had seen there at dawn. He would have seen the Regulars running away from the American Militia, racing desperately down that same road up which he had seen them, only a few hours before, march so proudly.

They were well-trained soldiers for battlefield fighting. They were brave men, used to the ups and downs of military life. But this was something entirely different from any fighting they had ever seen on battlefields. They were being fired at not by other well-trained soldiers drawn up in straight lines, loading and firing as their officers gave orders. These bullets which came zinging in, they could not see from where, were fired by the citizens of a whole province, who hated them, who needed no officers to tell them how to shoot.

Panting, running, falling, the Regulars retreated "like a flock of sheep chased by dogs," some American farmer said who saw them. Nobody had ever dreamed that red-coated British soldiers could ever be seen running wildly away from their enemies.

By night they were—those of them who still lived—back in Charlestown, safe in the protection of British cannon and the British army. All that night boats were ferrying them back to Boston.

Now the workingman who had been a silversmith was once more to ask himself the practical Revere question, "What does my country now need that I can do?"

What Work Now for Revere?
21

WHAT *was* needed by the small colonies, with little money, few soldiers, and almost no manufacturing, now starting to fight the most powerful nation and, so everybody thought, one of the finest regular armies in the world? Silversmithing was not one of the things needed by America. Paul Revere instantly gave up his own kind of work. For years to come, he shaped no more silver into beautiful cups and bowls and platters.

But he had handled metal for years. So he knew more about the nature of metals than men who had worked only in wood, as most Americans then did. Copper was needed by the colonists to sheathe their ships— copper in larger sheets than they yet knew how to make. Paul Revere began putting his mind on how to make copper in large sheets.

Money of their own was needed by the Americans. Paper money, banknotes. Paul Revere set his quick, practical mind, and those skillful hands of his, to learn how to engrave copper-plates to print banknotes.

Artillery was desperately needed by the Americans for their army. Paul Revere had been, twenty years before, a militia officer of artillery, and had learned all he could from study of the field-artillery of that expedition. He had not been able to learn much, but it was enough to prepare him to be an apt student when he was given a better chance to study. A French cannon-maker, very skilled in the manufacture of artillery, as the French were at that time, came over on his own to America, to help along the Revolution. He said he would teach his methods "to such persons as the State selects." And who was selected by the state to learn this new art, so important to the American Army? You guess. Paul Revere, of course.

Gunpowder—oh, how gunpowder was needed! The colonies had only the smallest amount. Compared to the Regulars, they were all sharpshooters. But guns can't be fired without powder. Paul Revere was asked

by American leaders if he would find out how gunpowder is made, and design and lay out plans for factories to manufacture it. He went all the way to Philadelphia to see a powder-making factory there. In one
day's visit (he was allowed to stay no longer) his quick
eye saw enough so that when he came back he was
ready to make drawings of the machinery needed to
manufacture it in Massachusetts.

That winter he lived in Watertown, not far from
Boston. Soon his family was with him. The people who
stayed inside Boston were mostly those Americans who
sided with the English, and of course the Regulars.
Paul and his wife wrote back and forth to each other, a
few hurried notes taken in and out secretly. In these,
they planned to get together outside Boston. At least
the family would be united.

All but that oldest boy, Paul. He was now nearly
sixteen years old. As his father had told him, he was no
longer a boy, a child, but another man in the family.
He was to stay in Boston and see if he could save the
little house, the furniture and the tools which made up
all the property the Reveres had. It was a big responsi-
bility to put on a boy, for nobody knew what was
coming next. Everybody thought that of course the
British would send their splendid navy racing across
the Atlantic from England to Boston, the ships loaded
with fresh soldiers, arms, food, money, and cannon for
their army there. Then they would be able to drive the
Colonial militia before them, as the militia had driven

the Regulars back from Concord. That was what looked likely. People who were on the British side expected, of course, that they were on the winning side.

But the Reveres stuck to the American side. Mrs. Revere got through the lines out to Watertown where her husband was. With her was Paul's old mother and all those children, except young Paul. There she set up housekeeping as best she could, making a good home for the Reveres, young and old, as she always did.

Of young Paul, left behind to guard the shop, they knew little. Boston people on the American side were almost completely separated that winter from those who stayed behind in Boston.

It was sometime in May, 1775, a month after the battle of Lexington, that Mrs. Revere and the children and their old grandmother joined Paul outside. Not until the next March were they to find out whether young Paul were alive, whether their house were still standing.

The American troops outside Boston during all those months were under General George Washington's orders, and he was as good as a general can be. But the best officer in the world can't get much fighting done by soldiers who know how to shoot but have only nine cartridges apiece. So General Washington had them dig—and that those everyday working Americans knew how to do. In a short time they had made a solid wall of earth ten miles long, which kept the English troops inside Boston from coming out to fight. On their side the British troops built up even higher walls, in some places thirteen feet high, made of heavy planks and great wooden beams. This kept the Americans outside Boston from going in to fight. Neither side could get at each other. Week after week, month after month, they waited.

All that time, Paul Revere worked as best he knew how at whatever was needed. He made copperplates for printing paper money. He made plans for that gunpowder factory. He studied and experimented as he tried to learn how to roll out copper in the big plates needed for sheathing American ships. Once during the summer, a Boston barber swam across the harbor to the Americans with news of all that was going on inside Boston. It was bad. There was nothing to eat but salt-pork and dry peas. Occasionally some fish. Never an egg. Never a vegetable. A captain, son of a wealthy English lord, said he had tasted fresh meat only twice in three months. Many people were sick. There were at least ten deaths every day. Sometimes thirty. The bells were no longer tolled for funerals. There were too many of them. Everybody was getting very thin—even the British army. *Even the officers!* For Great Britain did not succeed in sending supplies to the army now shut up in Boston. Not then. Not ever.

How was young Paul? The Reveres were anxious and sore-hearted about the boy. They were out in the farming land countryside seven miles from Boston. Plenty to eat there. If only they could send in some of their good food to the sixteen-year-old boy trying to take care of their little Boston home.

Later on, news came that one of Paul Revere's brothers had died. Smallpox was raging in Boston. Was young Paul still alive?

Young Paul's father kept steadily at work doing what needed to be done. He was getting on with the plans for manufacturing copper. It looked as though he would learn how. He did, and later became one of the first copper manufacturers in the United States, as in years to come he became one of the great foundrymen to make cannon.

Winter came. Inside Boston, life was harder and harder. In July fresh meat had cost a high price per pound. By December, it cost fourteen times as much. What little flour and dry peas were left were kept for the British soldiers. Oh, what was young Paul finding to eat?

Then, out there in Watertown, with all the firewood they needed, they heard that inside the besieged town the British troops were tearing down Boston churches and homes and using them for firewood. All the town of Charlestown was destroyed. Was their small home, all they owned in the world, still standing? Would they ever be able to go back to see it? Or would the big supply ships from England, expected any day, any hour, come thundering in with cannon firing, flags flying, bringing victory to the British?

Through this suspense, Paul Revere worked steadily on in the printing shop he had managed to set up, making copperplates, printing what the American side needed printed.

But we know how he loved his children, and we can imagine what a day it was for him when the Americans got hold of some big cannons, set them up on the heights across the bay from Boston, and began firing on the town. Then the British gave up waiting for relief to come from England, and took ship to sail away out of Boston harbor.

As they filed into their ships on one side of Boston, old Israel Putnam, now an American general, led the first American soldiers into the other side. And it was not long before the streets were filled with returned Boston families racing along to see who was left alive, whether their homes had been burned. Of that day, it has been said that "Boston was full of tears and joy," as each family found out what was left to them.

In the door of the beloved little Revere house stood a lanky sixteen-year-old boy. He was ghastly thin, his face was white and not at all clean. His dirty clothes hung on him in rags. But his eyes were proud as he waited for his father to come to see the shop unharmed, the plain small house still a home. Like his grandfather, Apollos Rivoire, like his father, Paul Revere, he had done what there was to be done. He had stuck it out. It was a good hour for him.

But was his family still alive? Was his father——? Would they come? He stood looking up and down the street filled with other people's families.

And then—there his father was, hurrying towards the old home—and his mother, coming more slowly, helping the grandmother along. And the brothers and sisters—grown so tall since he had seen them.

They saw him now, standing there in the door of the home he had saved for them. They saw him. Alive, yes—but skeleton-thin, white-cheeked—like a dead person—could that be their sturdy, broad-shouldered young Paul? He saw them. He waved his hand. He smiled. Yes, yes, it was their dear boy.

They began to cry. They began to laugh. They hurried in, all talking at the same time. "Quick, quick, Sara, open the food basket. Paul, oh Paul *dear*, here is some bread and butter. Fanny, give your brother the jug of milk. Where's that cold pork? Oh Paul, how thin you are! Here, take one of these apples!"

The Revere home, like Boston, was full of tears and joy. They stood in the shop, so excited that they could only laugh, and cry, and wipe their eyes, and begin to laugh again through their tears.

"Run along, children, don't you want to see the rest of the house? See if the baby remembers it?"

The younger children scampered through the familiar rooms, shouting and laughing, touching everything, sitting down on all the chairs. Mrs. Revere took one look at her husband and his big son, and went on into her own room, the center of their life, the kitchen, leaving the two menfolk alone.

Outside in the streets, crowds poured past, anxiously searching for their own, weeping in heart-break over their lost sons and daughters—or in loud joy to find them alive.

Inside the shop, by the well-beloved workbench, stood the dark-eyed, stocky, middle-aged man, his hand on his tall son's bony shoulder. "Paul, ——" he said, his dark eyes fixed tenderly on the boy's white face. "Oh, Paul——" He swallowed. Finally, "You did a good job, my son," he said.

And then, "Eat your bread and butter, son, and drink your milk. You need it. You're no more than bone." He pushed the boy into a chair. "Sit down, sit down. You look as though your legs were like cotton twine."

"Reveres know how to stiffen their legs," said the boy, through a huge mouthful of food. "What is there for us to do now, Father?"

Paul Revere turned his back on the past of his beloved skill, and faced the future. "We'll put our silver tools away—up attic—till later. Copper work is needed," he said. "I'll show you what I've found out about it. We can work together on that.

"And there's gunpowder to be made. Dr. Franklin in Philadelphia is at work getting saltpeter. What we must do here is to design the machinery. I'll show you what I've learned."